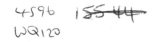

The Beginner's Guide to Fatherhood

D0620490

The Beginner's Guide to Fatherhood

How to cope with life before, during and after birth

COLIN BOWLES

Illustrated by Frank Rodgers

Fontana

An Imprint of HarperCollins*Publishers*

Fontana
An Imprint of HarperCollins*Publishers*,
77-85 Fulham Palace Road,
Hammersmith, London W6 8JB

A Fontana Original 1992
1 3 5 7 9 8 6 4 2

Text copyright © Colin Bowles 1992
Illustrations by Frank Rodgers

The Author asserts the moral right to
be identified as the author of this work

A catalogue record for this book is
available from the British Library

ISBN 000 637783 1

Set in Meridien and Gill Sans

Printed in Great Britain by
Hartnolls Ltd, Bodmin, Cornwall

For Lauren and Jessie:
long may you run

Contents

Introduction: Nouvelle Fatherhood

The fruit of your loins . . . will it turn out to be a lemon?

For years men did not see fatherhood as a very demanding role. Their function was quite simple: they were supposed to bring home the wage packet, get drunk on Fridays, hit the children when requested by their wives, and pay for their daughter's wedding. They spent the rest of the time in the garden shed making corner cupboards.

But times have changed.

Back in the late sixties, about the time when people started to worry about the ozone layer and read the list of ingredients on barbecue-flavoured crisps and say things like 'interpersonal relationships' and 'worst-case scenario', men discovered there might be more to manhood than scoring tries and discharging firearms at unarmed rabbits. Women actually demanded they take a hand in bringing up, rather than beating up, their own children.

Fatherhood was invented. Men found it was a bit more difficult than they thought.

This book is merely a guide, a grade-one primer. If you're a new father, or about to become one, it may give you some idea of what to expect, and you may perhaps find a few helpful pointers on what to do – and what not to do. If not, it may coax a few wistful smiles the next time you have a free moment – probably at about three in the morning, when your new son or daughter is finally asleep.

But more of that later.

Now I am not the classic, perfect, nouvelle father. Quite the reverse. I've made my share of mistakes and in the process I've learned a few things (usually too late). I never read up beforehand. I thought fatherhood would be a breeze.

And I'm still not sure whether preparation would have helped. Even if you enter fatherhood fully prepared and fully informed, fatigue and frustration will almost certainly cause you to lose your cool under pressure and forget everything when you need it most. You'll rant and rave and froth at the mouth and the whole situation will deteriorate and people will shout and cry and threaten. It will only be later on when you've calmed down that you'll realize what you should have done.

Then – and only then – will you know what it's like to be a real father. Congratulations!

Until then, here are a few pointers to be going on with . . .

CHAPTER I

A Brand New Concept

Or: too late now, sucker

Okay, fella, so you're going to have a baby. My God, do you realize what you've done? No, chances are, probably not.

Men come up with lots of different reasons for having children. Some say they want to carry on the family name. I have heard this from guys with surnames like Dorkfield and Titford and Pecker.

Or they say they want to have someone to look after them in their old age. This from a guy who has just registered Gramps into a local nursing home and has his furniture piled up on the Ford transit van outside, ready to take to the jumble sale on Saturday.

Other guys tell you they did it because they wanted to keep their marriage together. This is like starting a civil war in order to take the population's mind off the balance of payment figures.

Some men say it proves their masculinity. Especially if it's a boy. His wife is pregnant and suddenly he's Clint Eastwood with a smoking gun.

Others reckon they have a subconscious longing for immortality. Well, having children does not make you want to live for ever. In fact, most of the time in the first twelve months you'll wish you were dead.

Other men do it because their wives have talked them

into it. They tell their husbands they want a baby because it will fulfil them as a woman: as if spending twelve months in a housecoat with regurgitated milk stains on each shoulder makes them the re-incarnation of Julia Roberts.

Very rarely will you hear men say: 'Well, we decided to have children because my wife and I both did terrible things when we were younger and now we deserve to suffer.'

Most men get caught up in child-rearing sort of by mistake, or by default. The woman says she wants a baby so the guy says, 'Okay,' and hums to himself and carries on rebuilding the motor on his Morgan or cleaning his football boots or anti-fouling his forty-foot yacht, not realizing he has just agreed to give up all these things. He only realizes what he's let himself in for when it's too late.

There is something primal and irrational about reproducing. We are all amoebas at heart. When my wife and I decided to start a family, we were simply aware of a restlessness, a formlessness, a gap we needed to fill. We had bought a parrot the previous year but it had not turned out to be much of a tax advantage.

So we went ahead and got ourselves pregnant.

John Lennon was right: Imagine!

Children are basically a failure of the imagination. Men and women have children because they sit in candle-lit restaurants and imagine a tiny version of the baby Jesus wrapped in a pink chenille blanket that goo-goos at them and at whose cradle family and neighbours all come to worship like the three Magi. They imagine putting it to sleep at six o'clock every night in a nursery packed with musical mobiles and fluffy pink teddy bears.

They do not imagine a baby Jesus that goo-goos a foul-smelling mustard-like substance all over the pink chenille blanket. They do not imagine that having put the baby Jesus to sleep at six o'clock, they will then have to repeat

the performance every hour, on the hour, right through till breakfast. They do not imagine the toddler Jesus tearing the mobiles from the ceiling for recreation and using the teddy bears as weapons. They do not contemplate that one day family and friends might view their child not as much as Saviour of the World but as evidence of demonic possession.

Plus, they do not imagine the sacrifices. For example, you relinquish the right to finish a sentence. You forfeit watching the news for watching Care Bear videos. A good night's sleep is something you won't be getting again until about the time your superannuation's due. You also have to be prepared to sacrifice drinking leisurely cups of coffee in outdoor restaurants, admiring the view; you will give this up for bun fights in McDonalds watching your children being pushed off the recreational equipment by other people's immortalities.

What's up, Chuck?

But first comes pregnancy. Suddenly, the whole dynamics of being a husband changes too. *The Joy of Sex* is replaced on the bedside table by *The Heartache of Motherhood* and *Penthouse* is nudged out by *Mother and Baby* magazine.

When we were having our first daughter, I found that my wife suddenly became public property. Complete strangers smiled at her in the street. Not horny brickies or leering old men in plastic macs, but post office clerks in cardigans who asked her if she'd like a boy or a girl and little old ladies who approached her at bus stops and proceeded to tell her, uninvited, about their grandchildren.

My wife was no longer a sex object. She had become wholesome.

She hated it.

My wife – till then a warm, charming, easy-going woman – suddenly became difficult to live with. She blamed me for her morning sickness. She cried that she didn't really want the baby. She told me she was ugly and that I didn't love her any more. She accused me of escalating the situation in the Middle East. She became totally unreasonable.

In fact, for the first three months I handled being pregnant much better than my wife. Of course, vomiting every day could have had a negative effect on her outlook.

I married a teenage whale

But then, for the man, pregnancy does not really connect with reality. It's like thinking about end of year exams when you're only halfway through first term. It was only when she couldn't do up the top button on her jeans that we both started to realize the irrevocable nature of what we had done.

Even then, it does not really hurt the man until the credit

card statements start rolling in. Fatherhood involves going into the sort of shops you would not even have noticed before. There's a whole wardrobe of gear you'll need: cots, baby carriers, baby-changing tables, sweaters, socks, vests, booties, tops, blankets, plastic pants, baby bathtubs with pictures of Donald Duck on them.

And there are other things you've never even dreamed of. When Junior can sit upright you will need a safety seat for the car. They come in all models, like everything else: expensive; very bloody expensive; and junior executive. If you really love your child you'll get them the £150 junior executive club class with the cloth trim, arm rests and ashtray.

Even then, for some guys, it's still all a game. It's like humouring your wife in a second childhood: dollies all over again. The first time round, it took me about seven months to digest completely the fact that pregnancy was going to culminate in a real, live baby. It happened when we went to the beach and my wife had to dig a hole before she could lie on her belly, like a beached turtle. By this time we could not go more than ten paces from a lavatory. She could not get out of a chair without the help of half a dozen fit men and block and tackle.

Then, one day, her navel popped.

It was the cue to go to antenatal classes.

The Pillow Club

For years men never went near a labour ward. They hung around in waiting rooms with Woodbines clenched between their teeth. If they were smokers, they even lit them. When they were finally shown into the nursery, they handed the baby back to the midwife as if it was a ticking bomb, then went down the pub, were congratulated by all their mates for the way they paced up and down the waiting room smoking cigarettes and, in return, they bought the drinks all night until they spent all the money they had put aside for the pushchair.

Then women decided they would like to have their men beside them to help them through this ordeal and say 'push'. At first, this was only popular with John Lennon lookalikes from California who called their children Frisbee or Woodstock. Other men – the ones who had no intention of actually talking to their babies until they had started shaving – were opposed to the idea.

But it caught on anyway.

Antenatal classes were an introduction for men and women into the mysteries of reproduction.

Especially for men.

Our antenatal class consisted of a dozen other women who were going to have babies and men who were going to say push. Most couples were having their first baby, and you could pick them out easily: they looked enthusiastic. There were others who already had children. You could pick them out too: they looked fed up; also a little smug.

Maybe like they knew something we didn't.

Nah! Couldn't happen.

The miracle of twelve months' sleepless nights

All you need to qualify for an antenatal class is a positive pregnancy test and pillows. You need the pillows because you and your wife will spend a lot of time lying on the floor pretending to have babies together. This involves something called Breathing Exercises.

The antenatal class instructor will tell you that, by breathing a certain way, the woman can overcome a lot of the pain associated with childbirth. The theory is that she'll concentrate so hard on her breathing, she'll forget she's lying on her back with her legs wide apart while a foreign body tries to rip her uterus apart. The breathing technique, I hasten to add, was invented by a man.

At antenatal classes you will also watch videos of other women having babies. It's actually not too bad. The one we saw had Spanish guitar music playing in the background. It was all over in fifteen minutes. The man was a good 'push' shouter. The woman was a fair to average breather.

Then there were lectures and demonstrations. Now let me break this to you gently, I'd prefer you heard this first from a friend: the vagina is not all it's cracked up to be. In fact, having discussed it at length a number of times in childbirth classes, it has begun to lose some of its allure.

However, let me explain for novices the Miracle of Life. What happens is this: to start with, one of the woman's eggs hangs around in the ovum feeling premenstrual and moody and baiting all the other cells in the neighbourhood. Suddenly, all these little sperms come bursting in and rushing around all over the place looking for someone to mate with. It's just like a rugby club dance, in fact.

Eventually, one of them collides with the egg and, suddenly, you have the 'miracle of twelve months' sleepless nights'.

The cells start duplicating themselves and splitting into departments and sub-committees; every child is born with an inclination to work for the Civil Service.

Within three weeks, it has developed all the organs it requires to scream at the top of its lungs in supermarkets. After two months, it has grown all the parts it needs to destroy a compact disc player.

At the end of nine months, the baby is fully formed. Don't be put off by the fact that it actually looks more like an eight-pound monkey with skin the colour and texture of a boiled prune.

It may be a pruney monkey, but it will be *your* pruney monkey.

Ve haf vays of making you haf babies

This is your preparation for childbirth. Let me tell you this now, so you won't feel let down later on. Antenatal classes prepare you for the real thing like a trip to the chiropractor prepares you for being turned on the rack by the Spanish Inquisition.

The real thing invariably starts at around three in the morning. The signal is something a woman has, called a 'contraction'.

Even before our first daughter was born I suspected that the word 'contraction' was a euphemism, like 'passing on'. If it was called by its real name, 'disembowelment syndrome', for example, or 'the rack effect', women might stop having babies.

A contraction is a baby's notice to quit. Like eviction notices, they get increasingly severe as time passes.

Men have no conception of what it is like, if you'll pardon the pun. Carol Burnett explained it this way: 'If you want to know the feeling, just take your bottom lip and pull it up over the top of your head.'

After the first strong surge of disembowelment syndrome most couples race off to the hospital, headlights flashing, horn blaring. The baby will be born three weeks later.

The Texas Chainsaw Massacre

When our first daughter was born, I must admit to finding the breathing part a breeze. I held up my end, no problem. I breathed properly and I shouted 'push!' when they told me to. My wife, however, who had graduated with straight A's in breathing from antenatal classes, seemed to be having a little difficulty. On top of that, she had lost her sense of humour.

This did not surprise me, under the circumstances. I realized the video they showed us in antenatal classes was sadly inadequate as an introduction to the labour ward. If you want to give yourself a better idea, get yourself a copy of *The Texas Chainsaw Massacre*.

Standing up in the stirrups

If you decide to have your baby in a hospital, you basically entrust the doctors and nurses with the job of getting the baby out.

These people can also provide analgesics (painkillers). These days analgesia has been refined to the point where a woman can be wheeled into the delivery room a few seconds after the first twinge and not wake up again until after the kid has finished teething. She also loses all muscle control, which is why the doctor often has to use something that looks like bolt cutters to get the child out. It also means your monkey will not only have pruney skin but also a pointy head and a splitting hangover.

You may also come across something called an episiotomy. This is another euphemism. It entails slicing open the vagina with a pair of sharp scissors.

Now you understand why they call it an episiotomy.

You may find your good woman becoming a little cranky. After the fourth strong rack effect, breathing exercises will go out of the window. Your wife will groan in despair and you will cling to her hand like she has gone over a cliff and you are trying to pull her back. Which is in some ways exactly what has happened. But try and remember that the Missing Link also came into this world without a proper breathing technique and sooner or later nature will work things out.

She will then go into something called 'transition', which is a period of grace when your wife will loudly inform everyone that she has had it with the whole thing, she does not want a baby, she never did, it was this bastard's (that's you!) fault and she is now going to sleep. Shortly after, she will get the urge to push.

This is your big chance. You can yell 'push!' all you want. She is going to anyway, because she can't help herself.

The baby will come out next. As an onlooker you should remember this simple fact because it is sometimes easy to get the baby mixed up with the afterbirth. Babies are born blue and are covered with slime, and unless you have some experience in these matters you might think your wife just pushed out her liver.

The goochie-goochie syndrome

Things do improve, if only in the short term.

A few minutes after our first daughter was born, I picked

her up in my arms and a miraculous change had taken place. Lauren smelled like angel fluff and looked as if she was minted by Michelangelo. All the other babies in the ward still looked like skinned lizards to me. But that's the way it is. Fathers project all manner of perfection on to their daughters. It never occurs to you that you may have just sired Cyndi Lauper.

Father, forgive them

Children are like peanuts. Have one, and you can't stop. You don't want an only child, so you have another. Some people have a preference for a boy or a girl, so if they have two of the same sort they try again. And again. Before most men realize what they have done, they have fathered the Brady bunch.

You think the labour ward was bad? Your troubles have only just begun . . .

CHAPTER 2

Preparing for the Happy Event

Work out now!

Some couples prepare for having children by going to baby shops, reading Sheila Kitzinger and building extensions on their houses. This is completely the wrong approach. Parenthood is not just a matter of decorating a nursery and making more space. Raising offspring, like abseiling and karate, cannot be learned from a book.

The only way you'll ever learn to do it is by practice. But once you've got one of the little buggers, it's too late. You'll be too tired, physically, emotionally and spiritually, to learn anything new for at least five years.

You need to start working out straightaway.

Here's a training circuit you should incorporate into your life right now, twenty-four simple exercises that will help prepare you for the experience of being a father . . .

1 Go home. Pick up the paper. Read it for the last time. Move straight on to exercise 2 . . .
2 To discover what the nights are like, walk round the living room from about five in the afternoon till ten at night carrying a wet bag weighing approximately eight to twelve pounds. At ten o'clock, put the bag down, set the alarm for midnight and go to sleep.

Get up at twelve and walk round the living room again

– with the bag, of course – till one a.m.. Set the alarm for three a.m.. As you can't get back to sleep, get up at two and make a cup of coffee. Go to bed at quarter to three.

Get up at three when the alarm goes off. Sing songs in the dark till four a.m.. Put the alarm on for five. Get up, make breakfast.

Keep this up for five years. Look cheerful.

(Note: don't worry, hallucinating is normal.)

3 As all small children have a vital neuron missing in their brains making it impossible for them to agree to anything, you must practise a technique known as 'negative gearing'. That is, you gear every question you ever utter so that agreement requires a negative. Practise saying things like, for example: 'It's not that you don't not want to not go to bed, don't you?'

Master the technique or you won't not never make it through parenthood.

4 For some houseproud people, becoming a parent can be a bit of a shock. Children can be a little messy at times. To allay this trauma, try it out now and see if you can stand it.

First, smear Marmite on to the sofa and jam on all the curtains. Hide a fish finger behind the music centre and leave it there throughout the summer. Finally, stick your fingers in the flower beds, then wipe them clean on the walls. Cover over the stains with crayons.

There. How does that look?

5 Before you finally decide to go ahead, find a couple who already have children and berate them about their methods of discipline, their lack of patience, their appallingly low tolerance levels and the way they have allowed their children to run riot generally. Suggest ways in which they might improve their child's sleeping habits, toilet training and overall behaviour.

Enjoy yourselves. It will be the last time in your lives you'll have all the answers.

6 Dressing children, especially small children, is not as easy as it appears from a distance. To become really expert, buy an octopus and a string bag. Attempt to put the octopus in the string bag so that none of the arms hang out. **Time limit:** all morning.

7 Throw away *The Joy of Sex.*

8 Take an egg box and using only a pair of scissors and a pot of paint turn it into an alligator. Now take a toilet roll tube and using only Pritt and Alcan foil make a Christmas cracker. Finally, take a milk container, a ping-pong ball and an empty packet of Coco Pops and make an exact replica of Angkor Wat.

Congratulations. You have just qualified for the Play Group Committee.

9 Family cars are vital accoutrements for children. Sell your Mazda RX-7 and buy a Sierra estate. Wait! Don't just leave it out in the driveway spotless and shining. Family cars don't look like that.

Buy a triple-choc ice cream and put it in the glove box. Leave it there for a long time. Get a fifty pence piece and stick it in the cassette player. Snap off the console lid and the windscreen wiper control. Wrench off the side view mirrors. Mash a packet of chocolate biscuits down the back seats. Finally, take the garden rake and run it along both sides of the car.

There. Perfect.

10 Get a safety pin. Stick it in your thumb. Keep doing it until you no longer flinch at the pain. You are now ready to start changing babies' nappies.

11 Get dressed in shoes and a coat. Sit outside the toilet for half an hour tapping your foot. Walk out of the door. Come back in again. Go out. Come back in. Go out. Come back in again.

Go down the front path. Come back. Go back down the path. Walk very slowly along the street for five minutes. Stop to inspect minutely every cigarette end, piece of used chewing gum and dead insect along the way. Retrace your steps. Go back up your front path.

Now scream that you've had about as much as you can stand, until all the neighbours come out and stare at you. Give up and go back into the house. Do it all again a few minutes later.

Well done. You are now ready to take a small child for a walk to the shops.

12 Always repeat everything you say five times. Always repeat everything you say five times. Always repeat everything you say five times. *Can't you understand plain English??!* Always repeat everything you say five times. *For the last time, if I have to say this again I'm going to start getting angry!!* Always repeat everything you say five times.

13 Buy a blank cassette tape. Record someone saying 'Are we there yet?' on one side and 'How much further?' on the other. Every time you get in the car put the cassette in your tape player and play it at full volume continuously as you drive.

14 If, as a concerned and modern husband, you intend to be present at the birth, there are three things you can do:

a) Learn to say: 'There, there.'
b) Learn to say: 'Push' when someone tells you to.
c) Learn not to say: 'Why aren't you breathing the way they showed you in antenatal class?'

15 Go into your local supermarket. Take with you the nearest thing you can find to a pre-school child – a fully grown goat is excellent. If you intend to have more than one child, take more than one goat. Now take the child (goat) to the local shops, the DIY shop, or the off-licence, or wherever you frequent the most. Do not let the child (goat) out of your sight. Pay for everything the child (goat) eats or destroys.

Until you can accomplish this, do not even contemplate fathering children.

16 Untangle a mobile. **Time limit:** six months.

17 Buy a Taiwanese-made bicycle. Assemble it *exactly according-ing to the instructions.* **Time limit:** two years.

18 Make a Wendy house. **Time limit**: twenty-five years.

19 To get used to imagining how your wife will look, have her put on a pair of your socks. Buy her a terry-towelling housecoat. Stick a bean bag down the front and leave it there for nine months. After nine months, you can take out about ten per cent of the beans.

20 Go to the local chemist and tip the contents of your wallet out on the counter and tell the pharmacist to help himself. Then go to the doctor. Sign a blank cheque and hand it to him. Next, go to the supermarket and arrange to have your wages paid directly to their head office in London.

21 Hollow out a pumpkin. Make a hole in the side of the pumpkin roughly the size of a golf ball. Attach the pumpkin to a piece of rope and suspend it from the ceiling. Swing the pumpkin so that it sways from side to side in a two metre arc.

Now get a bowl of soggy Weetabix and attempt to spoon the Weetabix into the swaying pumpkin by pretending to be a jet plane. One hit out of ten will be considered a pass. Two out of ten is excellent.

Continue until half the Weetabix is gone. Tip the rest in your lap. You are now ready to feed a twelve-month-old child.

22 Toddlerhood is a very sensitive time. During this period most children become very insecure and tend to cling to their parents. To prepare adequately for this:

a) Buy a sandbag.
b) Fill it with approximately fifteen kilos of sand.
c) Tie it to your leg.
d) Leave it there for twelve months.

23 Go into a department store. Take the lift to the second floor and start browsing in the book department or reminiscing among the golf or football equipment . . . At the count of ten . . . Hurry! Quick! Find a toilet – *Now!!* **Time limit:** five and a half seconds.

24 Learn the names of every character from the Care Bears or Ninja Mutant Turtles. Leave the videos playing twelve hours a day. When you find yourself singing 'I wanna be a Care Bear' in the shower, you qualify as a good father.

CHAPTER 3

Rose, Or Any Other Name

Finding the right monicker for Monica . . .

The gestation period of the average human baby is nine calendar months. A mouse, on the other hand, is pregnant for just six weeks. Nature has arranged this discrepancy because a mouse does not have to choose a name for its baby.

Nine months, I contend, is just not long enough. Even after our daughter was born we were still at it. What were we going to call this new, and as yet anonymous, person? Andrea? Benita? Camille? Dixie? Emily? And so on through the alphabet.

After all, you can't take this responsibility too lightly. In a recent study in the United States, a group of teachers were given identical essays from fictional students to mark. It was found they consistently gave lower grades to fictional Elmers and Berthas than they did to imaginary Davids and Karens.

So from the very day of naming your baby, you have its future educational prospects in your hands. After long consideration, we finally settled on Einstein.

Then we changed our minds.

Denise could not come to school today: she was drunk

It was back to the baby books and page after page of names, each one with the original meaning in Greek, Latin, French, Gaelic or German written beside it in brackets. This was instructive in the way that Trivial Pursuit is instructive. Baby-name books give you the sort of information that is entertaining without ever being the slightest use.

We learned, for example, that we could call our child Athena (Greek for wisdom), but this seemed futile. For all we knew, she might be as dumb as a donkey. It might be nice to have a daughter who was all-gifted (from the Greek), but I still wouldn't call her Pandora. The only Pandora I ever knew wore a leather jacket and was gifted at rolling her own cigarettes and drinking straight from a vodka bottle. And why would someone call their child Denise when they discovered that it meant (from the French) 'adherent of Dionysius, Goddess of Wine'? What sort of parent aspires to a toddler who goes to the refrigerator and helps herself to the Beaujolais?

It's Greek for work, rest and play

I also learned from the baby-name book that our Christian names are (brace yourself for this one) the names we are christened with. It seems that up until the sixteenth century the church exercised ultimate authority over the naming of children at the christening, refusing to baptize any child with a 'heathen' name. Babies could, therefore, only be called after saints or martyrs. Consequently, handles like Zarathustra, Mars and Judas became less popular.

The 'Domesday Book' of the eleventh century reveals that choices were much simpler back then. There were only about twenty boys' names in currency, and about the same number for girls. There were no Jasons or Kylies or Taos or Desirees or Sabras or Jays or Tods or Tymons. If you were a girl you could be an Agnes, Cicely, Elizabeth or a Catherine; boys were either John, William, Thomas, Richard or Henry. Imagination only came into play in the choice of nicknames. Like Richard – the Lionheart; William – the Conqueror; Henry – the Eighth.

A Deadly Blanchwort by any other name

As the church lost its stranglehold over the individual, people began to bestow less conventional names on their offspring. Our generation is cursed with choice. My grandparents solved their problems at the outset by deciding to name all their female children after flowers. First there was Rose, then Iris, then Poppy, closely followed by Ivy, Violet and Lily. Unfortunately, their passion outlasted their imagination. By the time kids number thirteen and fourteen came along (they sired a preponderance of girls) Gramps and Granny were mentally as well as physically exhausted. I was the only kid on the block with an auntie called Deadly Blanchwort.

My own parents were a little more imaginative. They chose names it was difficult to shorten. They reasoned that this way we could get called by our proper names and not by common diminutives. So they avoided Thomas, Richard or Harold. They didn't want us to be any Tom, Dick or Harry.

Their reasoning was sound up to a point, but in my experience it's better to have a name you can shorten. Kids with short names don't get burdened with execrable nicknames. My sister, for example was called Bernadette. A pretty name and not easy to truncate. (Well, there's

'Bern' and 'Bernie' but my mother baulked at those.) Then Bernadette went to school.

As my parents had suspected, the other kids couldn't abbreviate the name to their satisfaction. So they called her Dopey instead.

Get thee to a nunnery, Porky

When Helen and I set out on our naming quest, we found there were other factors to be considered. For instance, as a parent you have a responsibility not to make your child a figure of fun. If you choose a name that's a touch outrageous, you need to have a very special child to carry it off successfully. Friends of ours have a nine-month-old baby who looks like a replica of the Michelin man. She was born that way, poor kid. When her parents take her nappy off, her cellulite drops from the hips in scallops and her knees disappear.

They called her Ophelia.

That decided us. Desiree and Ophelia and Sabrina and Chantelle were definitely out. We were also aware we had to watch out for unintended puns and word gags. I went to school with a boy called Martin Head. His middle name was Terence. He appeared on the school roster as M.T. Head. Then there was Barry Orpington: or B.O. as his satchel and sports gear described him. My wife says she knew a boy called Wright Paine. My sister-in-law went to school in Muswell Hill with a Jewish boy called Oylie Pecker.

You get my point.

Give peace a chance

The baby-name book also warned us to remember that a great name for a baby might not be such a great name for an adult. For example, back in the flower-power sixties,

Peace Love Harmony Groovy was a pretty, though slightly precocious, name for a petite, blonde, three-year-old girl. Such a name could seem unintentionally ironic for a harassed thirty-five-year-old mother of three going through a divorce. Imagine straggle-haired Peace screaming abuse at her husband in the Telford Family Court as she battles over who gets the house.

Think of all those baby Karmas that were born back then. How will someone called Karma react to menopause? How will a Woodstock handle baldness?

She was born on Remembrance Day, so we called her Trenchis

These are all things to be considered. So we had narrowed our choices. We needed a name that:

a) Could be shortened
b) Would not offend future tutors
c) Was not too outrageous
d) Did not contain any puns or sight gags
e) Did not contain the words Peace, Love or Harmony

So what did that leave? Well, some people name their children after relatives. It's why you still sometimes meet five-year-olds called Albert, Henry, Agnes or Beatrice. Personally, I don't see the point. If everybody named their children after their own parents, we'd never make any progress at all. Playgroups and kindergartens would be crawling with runny-nosed sprogs called Sigisbert and Ethelred the Unready. Someone has to break the chain.

Some friends advised us to wait until we actually saw the baby. 'Something will come to you the first time you see it,' they said, 'something apt.' Let me tell you right now that that is very bad advice. If I'd followed it our daughter would have gone through life as 'E.T.'.

Other alternatives suggested to us were to pick a name based on the timing of the birth. Like May, for example, or Tuesday. In fact, this idea nearly solved all our problems. Our baby was almost born on Easter Sunday. We nearly called her Bunny. As it was she missed by two days and we thought Third Quarter of the New Moon was a bit of a mouthful.

Yes, but we can't call her Chipping Sodbury

The other idea suggested to us was to contrive a name from the place where our baby was born. It seemed a novel suggestion at the time, and ripe with promise. I remembered once meeting an American Madison and an English girl called Dover. In Australia, there are even girls called Adelaide.

As it was we nearly settled on Otis because that was the

manufacturer's name on the lift in the labour ward where our daughter finally made her appearance. But it didn't seem to quite suit a girl. Especially with Maximum Load Eight People as a middle name.

Then someone else suggested we create our own name. Some friends called Neville and Valerie had done just that and called their children Neva and Vane. A nice idea, but it didn't really work for us. Colin and Helen are hard names to work with. With a bit of thought we finally came up with Colen. Or Helin. Take your pick.

Faith, Hope and Charity

By now we were getting desperate, so we cast around for other ideas. Helen read somewhere that some people choose names after an aspiration or an ideal: names like Faith, Grace, Hope or Bliss. This sounds fine but these people forget that the innocent pink bundle they now hold in their arms will one day turn into a raging, spit-fisted toddler. Then they will find themselves storming around the supermarket shouting profanities like: 'Where is my Faith?' and 'I've had just about enough of Charity!' and 'I'm going to murder Hope!'

She's been 235717 long enough

So after all this soul-searching we are still undecided. At the moment we are toying with Anne (Hebrew: graceful; mercy or prayer) and Shannon (Gaelic: girl from the island of Shan with a laurel in her hair and an adjustable spanner in her back pocket). Whatever we choose, I suppose we'd better make up our minds soon. We've mulled this over for long enough, I think. Time's running out. We can't procrastinate for ever.

She starts high school next year.

CHAPTER 4

Charting Your Progress

What to expect and when to expect it

It's too late now. The baby is born. There is no turning back. What awaits you in the coming weeks, months, years . . . ?

The following may be a helpful guide as you check your child's progress and give you some idea of what to expect as you embark on this great adventure called fatherhood . . .

One day:	The child is born. You promise yourself you are going to be a great father. You are not going to repeat your own parents' mistakes. You will not resort to shouting, smacking, bribery, wheedling and cajoling as a means of controlling your child's behaviour.
One week:	You take your child home from the hospital. You discover that a strong stomach is more important to a new parent than wisdom.
One month:	You look up the name of your local doctor in the phone book.
Two months:	Your local doctor reassures you that cradle cap isn't a form of leprosy.
Four months:	Your local doctor now knows you and

	your wife so well he calls you both by your first names.
Six months:	Your doctor's receptionist now knows you both so well she calls you by your first names.
Eight months:	Your local doctor's other patients now know you so well they call you both by your nicknames.
Nine months:	Your baby takes its first steps.
Nine months and one day:	You make your first house contents insurance claim.
Ten months:	Your child eats its first box of Kleenex.
Eleven months:	Your child learns to put together Lego.
Eleven and a half months:	Your child learns to take apart the CD player.
Fifteen months:	You build your fifteen-month-old a sandpit. He eats it.

One and a half years:	Your child goes through the 'clingy' stage. Treats you like a total stranger (this is good preparation for teenage years) but grabs your wife's leg and won't let go.
Two years:	Your child lets go.
Two and a half years:	Your child learns to talk.
Two and three quarter years:	Your child learns to talk too much.
Three years:	You hire a babysitter and go out and eat at a candle-lit restaurant together for the first time in three years. You spend the evening discussing potty training.
Three and a quarter years:	You and your wife receive a personal letter of gratitude and appreciation from the company that makes Wet Ones.
Three and a half years:	You finally work out how to fold and unfold the baby buggy. Your baby grows out of the baby buggy.
Three years and nine months:	Your child makes his first unassisted visit to the toilet in the middle of the night.
Three years and ten months:	Your child makes his first unassisted visit to the room he *thought* was the toilet in the middle of the night.
Four years:	Your child starts play group. Always the interested father, you go along. You learn to make an alligator out of egg boxes and green paint while your child plays on a climbing frame.
Four and a half years:	Your wife suffers fainting spells. This often happens the first time women see their son picking scabs off his knees and eating them. Sympathize. Don't tell her you did the same thing right up to high school.
Five years:	Your child starts school and comes home and tells you everything he/she did that day at school — for the last time.

Five and a half years:	Your child learns to count and uses this new skill to demonstrate that she has been given more disgusting peas than her sister.
Six years:	Your child invites the rest of her class round for her sixth birthday party.
Six and a quarter years:	You and your wife finish cleaning up the mess.
Six and a half years:	Your child asks for help with his homework for the first time. They're doing history and he wants to know if you'd heard of something called The Beatles.
Six and three quarter years:	Your child requests that pocket money be linked to the R.P.I..
Seven years:	Shouting, smacking, bribery, wheedling and cajoling have become your sole means of controlling your child's behaviour.
Eight years:	Childless couples start pointing out all the things you're doing wrong. Your father spends all his time gloating.

There, that doesn't seem so bad, does it? I bet you thought parenting was going to be really tough. But don't get complacent, that was just the easy part. From here on they say it starts to get really difficult . . .

CHAPTER 5

Nappy Days

The good, the bad and the dirty

I don't consider myself a particularly squeamish sort of person. The sight of blood doesn't worry me a bit; I've skinned and gutted rabbits; I even worked in advertising for a while. But the one thing I can't stand is a dirty nappy.

This is a bit of a handicap if you plan to have children. Forget what everyone tells you about patience, tolerance, kindness and wisdom being the most important qualities for a new parent. What you need most is a strong stomach.

Forget what people tell you about babies' nappies not smelling until they progress on to solids. This is a load of crap – if you'll excuse the expression and the word-play. They still smell. What people mean is that nappies don't become really smelly – really gut-churningly, toe-curlingly, nauseatingly, Oh-my-God-I-think-I'm-going-to-throw-up smelly – until they're weaned.

To give credit where credit is due, you will never hear a woman complain the way a man does about dirty nappies. Why is this? It could be that women have an underdeveloped sense of smell, but men who smoke or drink Guinness and then fart in bed have disproved this theory. It could be that, beneath the stubble and scars and Barbarian's rugby shirts, men are basically wimps.

Whatever the reason, new fathers should remember one

thing. Unless they work in an abattoir and are used to noxious odours or have a severe cocaine habit and have seared away all their nasal passages, they should take certain precautions before becoming parents.

You have been warned.

The Pampers calypso

Picture the scene. Your two-year-old daughter appears at your bedroom door. It is soft dawn and her brown curls are tousled from sleep; she has a cherub's smile and looks Charles Dickens cute. With her pink bunny clutched under one arm she is quite irresistible and so you invite her to get into bed with you. You and your wife cuddle up to her dreamily. Suddenly, neither of you can breathe.

One of the most insidious developments of the equal-responsibility New Fatherhood concept is something called Your Turn. As when it's Your Turn to change a nappy.

I'll be honest with you. I don't want you to publish this or anything but, between you and me, I consider it the father's prerogative to get out of changing nappies any way he possibly can. Pretend you're sick. Pretend you can't smell anything. Claim a bad back. Consistently make the nappy too loose so it always falls down and your wife suspects you of incompetence. This sort of acquired inadequacy is what New Fatherhood is all about. But if all else fails, you'll need to acquire a technique for changing dirty nappies.

I call mine the Jacques Cousteau method.

Dive, dive, dive

During my short and unspectacular career as a father I have discovered there is only one way to change a nappy. First, you have to block the nostrils and, second, you have to find an alternative air source.

One of the things I do when I want to get away from it all is go scuba diving. (If it's a choice between a four-year-old's birthday party and the bends, I'll take the bends anytime.) I discovered early on that a mask and snorkel is a pretty versatile piece of equipment and can be absolutely invaluable when changing a nappy. You can't smell a thing through the mask, and the snorkel draws the air straight from the ceiling.

In really bad cases – when the child has been eating snails, for example, or has a gastric attack – I use the air tank and regulator as well.

A pair of gardening gloves is useful also. I normally use these for taking lobster, but they can double effectively as vital protection when dealing with a pre-loved and fully-loaded Pampers.

My daughters both quickly got over their apprehension

of the mask and accepted this as normal behaviour. They would tap on the tempered glass and grin at me and play with the snorkel while I undid the pins.

There are hazards, however. One day I was just getting into the business end of the operation when the doorbell rang. I turned off the tap and, holding gardening gloves aloft like a surgeon, I ran to the front door and opened it with my elbows.

The Mormons.

They took one look, screamed and jumped on their Raleighs. Moments later, they disappeared up the street, sparks flying from their bicycle clips.

I'd forgotten to take the mask off.

I went back to the laundry, finished changing my daughter's nappy, took off the mask and snorkel, went to the door, explained the misunderstanding to the Police Tactical Response Group who had responded to the Mormons' emergency call, and went back to bed.

Pass the parcel

I know I'm not alone in suffering from Pamperphobia. Once we were at a dinner party at a friend's place. Their two-year-old woke up at about ten, came trotting into the lounge and plonked himself on his mother's lap. Trying to ignore the sudden change to the room's atmosphere, she passed him to her husband, who patted the child, sniffed, and passed him back.

She gave the child a kiss and handed him back. He patted Junior on the head and threw him back at his wife. She bounced him on her knee, realized with horror what she had done, and gave him back to her husband. And so it went on, this game of parental brinkmanship, both of them trying to pretend they hadn't noticed a thing, while the guests dropped like flies.

Of course, my sympathies went to the father. He had never been diving in his life and didn't possess any diving gear. How can you expect a man to change a nappy without a scuba mask? It can't be done.

CHAPTER 6

Eat Your Greens!

A guide to good nutrition

Most parents worry endlessly about their child's nutrition. This is pointless: it's like worrying about what's going on in Iran. It's probably unhealthy but there's nothing you can do about it.

The fact is, a child's tastes are quite different from an adult's. A child loves extremes: the extremely sweet and the extremely disgusting. There is an old joke: what's the difference between broccoli and mucous? The answer, of course, is that kids can't stand the taste of broccoli. When it comes to nutrition, this is the basic problem. A kid will always prefer the snail to the salad it arrived on.

Kids, however, will get through childhood well enough provided there is enough food left around, although the type of food they eat may not always be quite what you would choose for them. They prefer crayons to cauliflower, hand cream to natural yoghurt. A child could happily survive for years on Mars bars and whatever it could gnaw off its own fingernails.

So here's a quick guide to the nutritional value of some of those foods you maybe never considered.

Snails

Snails are a compact and readily available food source, and most crawling infants adore them. They can be crushed with the fist and eaten as a crunchy snack, or sucked like a sweet until dry. They contain no sugar, so parents need not worry about dental decay. Neatly packaged and easy to carry (they will fit inside most nappies) they're the sweet most children can eat between meals without ruining their appetite . . . though they may ruin yours when you discover the tell-tale slime trail on the chin.

Dirt

Dirt and soil are excellent sources of trace minerals and roughage. However, the consumption of blue metal, road gravel and hunks of displaced bitumen should be discouraged.

Pumpkin

A child will not eat anything that's green on principle. (Green popsicles are always the last to go.) The 'won't eat green' rule also applies to pumpkins, which are vegetables and, therefore, considered green even though they are orange. This rule also applies to carrots.

Parents try many ways of forcing a child to eat pumpkin. The preferred way is for the mother to mash it up into a goo then give it to the father and tell him to feed it to the child. Fathers, being inventive, playful and somewhat stupid when it comes to children, then put the orange goo on a spoon and pretend it is an aeroplane and the child's tongue is the runway. This is very entertaining for the child, who will put on the landing lights but then fog in at the last minute.

The ritual is self-defeating anyway. Should you manage to force half a teaspoon of mashed pumpkin down the child's throat, he or she will instinctively sick it up, thereby also aborting the three token peas you forced down in exchange for a promise of a plate of ice cream afterwards.

Cereals

Breakfast cereals contain plastic toys, special offers, picture cards and lots of sugar and are, therefore, in a child's opinion, an excellent form of nutrition. From a nutritionist's point of view most breakfast cereals are also a great form of roughage: provided the child eats the cardboard box they come in.

Peas

Peas are green and come under the 'won't eat green' rule that is mandatory in all healthy pre-school children. However, parents believe that peas are good for children, even though they have been dyed emerald with chemicals and kept in suspended animation at the back of the freezer for four years behind a forgotten packet of beefburgers. Most parents are willing, therefore, to trade off five peas against an offer of chocolate pudding for sweet.

The most important aspect of the pea is that it is educational. A child who shows no interest in mathematics at school will quickly learn to count up to thirty in order to establish that he does not have more peas on his plate than his big brother.

Sand

It has been calculated that most healthy children will eat approximately their own weight in dirt and sand by the time they are ready to go to nursery school. This does them no harm at all, and also gives the worms and snails something to live in before passing in to the duodenum.

Some restraint should be exercised with sand however, as it tends to have an effect on disposable nappies similar to sand-blasting, rendering them totally ineffective.

Nail parings

Most school-age children carry their own snacks around with them to get them through long and boring mathematics and history lessons. If you clip a child's nails, for example, you are depriving them of a vital snack food which they can nibble on all day. The same goes for toenails in really dexterous five-year-olds, and little girls can find vital trace elements in longish hair.

Caterpillars

Caterpillars are the one exception to the 'won't eat green' rule and are a premium source of nutrition. They are bite-sized and not at all messy, like chocolate. The usual method is to bite off one end and suck out the goodies, like

an popsicle. You will know if your child has been eating caterpillars because you will find the skins in the nappy the next morning. Alternatively, you will see a butterfly emerge from that part of the anatomy incapable of facial expression.

Books

Books may be eaten quite safely, in moderate amounts, as a between-meal snack. Too many can lead to addiction, however. If you find your child gnawing their way through the *Encyclopaedia Brittanica* or, worse, a James Michener novel, consult your doctor.

Or your librarian.

Sniffs

Prepare yourself to face the horrible truth. Sniffing to a child is merely another form of snacking. This is the real reason children will not eat when they have a cold. *They are full up.*

Cigarette ends

Cigarette ends are potentially harmful, so children should be discouraged from eating them: especially if they have found them down a drain.

Crayons, ink, etc

Most crayons and ink are okay to snack on during the day, though they have little nutritional value. If you want to discourage the habit buy your children only green and orange ones and tell them they are made from pumpkin and broccoli.

Broccoli

Broccoli, along with carrots, pumpkin, lettuce, and other vegetables and fruits, has excellent nutritional value. The best way to get your children to eat broccoli is to leave some behind the fridge for six months and allow them to discover it for themselves. It is then impossible to stop them eating it.

Conclusion: a child's just desserts

Don't lose too much sleep over some of the things your children eat. Most of them will get over this stage and grow up to be normal, healthy adults. One day, they will be able to go into fancy restaurants and order capably from the menu, rather than suck at the edges, and eat expensive foods.

Like snails, for instance . . .

CHAPTER 7

The Gender Agenda

The little bit of tissue issue

Two daughters do not constitute a large family and I'm told that, all in all, we're lucky to have a preponderance of females. I admit, there are obvious advantages in having girls. The main one that springs to mind is that girls do not shout 'Cowabunga!' and kick you in the groin when you're not looking. (Well, Jessica does, but there are exceptions to every rule.)

I was happy to accept whatever I got. As long as they were healthy, had all their fingers and toes, and I didn't have to change their nappies. (Two out of three isn't bad.)

But to some men the sex of the child really matters. They have to have a son to play football with or they insist on having a daughter to dote on. If they don't get what they want they keep playing ovary roulette until fortune provides, or their wives throw their hands up in exhaustion and move the wardrobe in front of the bedroom door until they can organize a hysterectomy.

Contrary to what you may have heard, little boys and little girls *are* different. Social conditioning and parental input can exaggerate these differences, but Nature and genetics have already determined that they cannot be the same.

You can try not to be sexist, but you may have only

limited success. When my oldest daughter was two, for example, I bought her a big Tonka truck. She used it as a pram for her cabbage patch doll.

Differences will quickly become apparent in their hobbies and interests and play. Boys collect mutant lifeforms from ponds and pull wings off flies and stick them down ants' nests. Little girls play with Barbie dolls and think washing up is a game.

Boys scream and bang their heads against walls when they can't get their own way. Little girls whine. Like thiiiiiiiiiiiiiiiiiiiiiiiiiiiiiiiiiiis. The difference between little boys and little girls is the difference between emotional blackmail and psychological torture.

Little boys are disgusting because they wipe their noses on their sleeves. Little girls use their skirts.

Little boys have a fascination for obscenity from a young age. Ask my daughter what the magic word is and she'll tell you it's 'thankyou'. Ask my nephew for the magic word and he'll tell you it's 'fuck'.

It is easier to teach girls bathroom etiquette. It is impossible – almost – for little girls not to pee straight. We have good friends with sons who spend all summer hosing down the toilet floor. Their bathroom smells like Jakarta. They tried putting a ping-pong ball down the loo and getting their sons to aim at it, but that ploy was abandoned when they found them playing with it in the garden.

'But, mum,' the older boy protested, 'we promise to put it back afterwards.'

Little girls will want to have their nappies changed. Little boys will happily squat in their own excrement for days. When it hardens they will use it as building blocks.

This trait for slovenliness becomes more endearing as they get older. They are easier to take out and much easier to dress. Boys don't care what they wear. To a small boy, it is a matter of complete indifference whether he is wearing overalls by Oshkosh and Weebok running shoes or a flour sack and gumboots.

With girls, it's different. We knew Lauren might be a problem right from the start. When she was two she pulled on her mother's skirt one day and said: 'Why am I wearing this nappy? I hate this nappy. It's frayed.'

For fathers, girls are easy to love, easy to indulge, less easy to play with. Most fathers baulk at plaiting Barbie's hair, re-arranging her underwear or slipping Ken into his new pink jumpsuit. Boys want to play football, or help in the workshop, girls less so. But sons can be difficult: as they get older, competition often sets in. If Dad has a business or a farm as soon as the son knows everything – when he's about thirteen – he wants to take over. Farmers have to be careful when they're standing near their combine harvesters. It's a terrible temptation for their sons. One little push and the acreage is *theirs*.

Probably the best thing we can do for our children, boys or girls, is to examine from the very day they are born, our innermost expectations. Why did we want that cherished son? What was so important about having a girl?

Are we prepared to accept them for what they are – or is there a hidden agenda for their gender? Is there a role we expect them to play out? Have we already set the benchmark for their lives?

I believe there are two traps we fathers should be wary of: pigeon-holing our daughters and trying to re-live our pasts through our sons.

Don't assume, just because your little girl likes playing with Barbie, that her ambitions don't extend beyond a C pass in maths and early motherhood. Don't forget that these days Barbie drives a pink Corvette (the insurance alone would be worth a fortune), has a filofax next to her pool lounger, a briefcase and a wallet full of credit cards. Just try and encourage her to keep away from toy-boys like Ken.

Equally, just because you always wanted to play on the wing for England, or win a gold medal for boxing at the Olympics, or go to Oxford, don't assume your son will too.

Make room for his own dreams and goals and ideals.

On the other hand, do your best if he talks about becoming a property developer.

Someone once said that fatherhood was one of the most creative things a man can ever do with his life. I don't believe it. Fatherhood is about discovery. Your task is to help someone else find their own style, define their own dreams, decide on their own values, not to create a Frankenstein's monster for yourself.

By the way, when Lauren grows up she wants to be the sugarplum fairy.

CHAPTER 8

The Truth, the Whole Truth . . .

Lies my toddler told me

Someone once said that honesty is the best policy and we have tried to teach our children the virtue of always telling the truth. But truth has a down side: if you are going to be one of those fathers who teaches his children that they should *not no way* never lie, you had better be aware of it.

I cannot tell a lie – it was her!

When our eldest daughter first went to school, she quickly learned how to write. I knew she had been learning how to write because one day I went into her room and found . . . MI NAME IS LAUREN. I LYK CATS . . . scrawled on the wall in red crayon.

'Who did this?' I screamed at her.

'Not me,' she said, looking me right in the eye. 'It must have been Jessie.'

Jessie, who was not yet three at this stage, was appalled that she had been accused of such a heinous crime. She drew the line at playing frisbees with compact discs.

'Your little sister can't write,' I said, trying to stay calm. 'I know it was you. Why did you do it?'

She gulped, but continued to stare me down. 'Jessie told me to,' she said.

Later on, after the yelling and screaming had died down a bit, we had a little talk about honesty.

'You should always tell he truth,' I told her. 'No matter what. Do you understand?'

'Always?'

'Always,' I said. I really felt I was getting somewhere. What a fantastic father.

Always tell the truth

My wife's older brother, Mike, was staying with us for a while. A while – make that four months. He had separated from his wife and had decided to travel around the country to get away from her divorce lawyer. He had landed on our doorstep with a travel bag in one hand and half a bottle of cheap red wine in the other and asked to be let in. He had then taken up residence in the caravan in the backyard.

One Sunday afternoon, we decided to go to the beach. 'Unka Mikie', as the kids had christened him, decided to get out of bed and join us.

'Poo,' Lauren said as he climbed into the back of the car. 'You stink.'

'It's just the garlic,' Mike said, looking uncharacteristically abashed. 'I eat a lot of garlic. It's good for colds.'

'Dad says it's because you don't ever wash.'

I could feel Unka Mikie's eyes burning a hole in the back of my head. I busied myself adjusting the wing mirror. There was a long silence, broken only by Jess repeating the word 'poo' about fifty times and giggling.

'Well,' my wife said as we reversed out of the drive, 'it's a nice day for the beach.'

When always is just mostly

Later on, with Mike safely back in his caravan – sulking perhaps, or merely having a nice rest after an exhausting couple of hours lying on the beach – I tackled Lauren on the subject of When Not To Tell the Truth.

'But you said always,' she protested.

'Almost always. You have to use tact.'

'What's tact?'

'We'll tell you when you're a big girl,' my wife said. 'You're too young to understand.'

'If she's old enough to ask the question, she's old enough to deserve an answer,' I said. 'Tact is when you don't tell the truth so as not to hurt someone else's feelings.'

'So should I always tell tact to Unka Mikie?'

'Yes.'

'Till when?'

'Not for much longer,' I said. 'If that parasite doesn't go soon I'm going to chuck him out.'

The conversation with my daughter ended there because I started having another conversation with my wife. A very loud one.

When mostly is just sometimes

Next morning, I was out in the garden and I saw Lauren go into Mike's caravan. I heard him telling her about all the exciting places he had visited – his brother's in Birmingham – and his plans to visit some even more exciting ones.

'When?' she asked him.

'One day,' Mike said.

'Better make it quick. Dad says he's going to chuck you out soon. But not because you smell,' she added quickly, possibly remembering the eulogy on Tact. 'Because you're a parasite. What's a parasite?'

Later that morning, Lauren and I had another discussion about honesty.

'You should never tell the truth for someone else,' I told her.

'Well, when can I tell the truth?'

'When I tell you to!'

When sometimes is once too often

Next day, Unka Mikie left to visit some more exciting places in the world (his sister Gemma in Dorking). We gave him a lift to the bus station.

'Good luck, Mike,' I said.

'Thanks for having me,' he said.

'It was a pleasure,' I said. 'Any time.'

That night as I was tucking her into bed, Lauren asked:

'Dad, what's a hypocrite?'

'Where did you hear that word?'

'It's what Mum said you were when you were saying goodbye to Unka Mikie.'

'Is that so?'

'What's a hypocrite?'

I thought about it for a moment. 'I'll tell you when you get a big girl,' I said. After all, she was probably too young to understand.

So be careful what you teach your children. Honesty can be a dangerous game. And ain't that the truth.

Things to remember:

1 You should teach your children always to tell the truth.
2 This is not always true.
3 So you should try to teach them tact.
4 You will fail miserably.
5 So you should at least help them to lie better.

Questions to think about:

- Should I have ignored the writing on the wall and left it for my wife to sort out? Illustrate your answer with diagrams.
- This whole sorry episode was her brother's fault. Tick the box if you agree: ☐
- In that case, should I have made him walk to the bus station?

CHAPTER 9

Catch Me, Daddy

The do's and don'ts of domestic violence

I want to talk to you right now about domestic violence. Look, I know it's a sensitive subject, but it has to be brought out into the open. Before one of us fathers gets seriously injured.

By one of our children, of course. There is nothing anyone can teach children about violence. Children should be born with a warning stamped on their chubby little pink bottoms: RAISING THIS INFANT IS A HEALTH HAZARD. For any foolhardy young men out there who are thinking of becoming fathers, here are a few words of advice that might help you survive.

1. Always leave a mattress on the toilet floor until your children are at least four.
When our eldest daughter was three years old and was just learning how to use a toilet, I broke a small bone in my wrist. She was leaning forward, her hands holding the edge of her skirt, trying to watch herself wee. This altered her centre of balance quite radically. Fortunately, I happened to be passing the toilet just in time to see her execute a full one hundred and eighty degree somersault on the toilet seat. By diving forward at full stretch, I managed to catch her head, soccer-goalkeeper fashion, a few inches from the floor.

If I had expected profound gratitude, I was to be sorely disappointed. Instead, she screamed at me for scaring her and yelled for her mother. She wouldn't come near me for days.

I couldn't have picked her up anyway. The arm was in plaster for six weeks.

2. Never lie around in bed in the mornings.

Fathers lying around in bed are openly inviting their children to jump on them. All young children enjoy this, especially when their father is half asleep and unable to defend himself. Not only that, they will always somehow manage to jump on your groin. Even when you're lying on your stomach. It's uncanny, but it's true.

3. Buy a pair of steel-capped boots. And don't take them off.

Especially if you have daughters. For some reason, little girls will only come up and talk to you when you are sitting down in your stockinged feet. At these times, particularly if it's going to be a long conversation, they like to stand on something warm and soft, such as your foot. They will only do this when they have shoes on. When they are in position they pirouette. On their heels. Then they jump up and down. Then they ask you why there's water in your eyes.

'Catch me, Daddy!'

Excuse me a moment . . .

That reminds me of the fourth thing.

4. Never teach them to play 'Catch me, Daddy!'

A few months ago, I showed my youngest daughter how to jump off the coffee table. I would then make a big play of catching her. Unfortunately, she liked the game so much that she has forgotten to stop playing it and has graduated to leaping off pianos, washing machines and the mezzanine floor.

She likes playing it most when I'm about thirty feet away on the other side of the room. Unless you have the reflexes of a slip fielder and the agility of an aerobics instructor, leave this game to the professionals. One of you could get hurt.

5. Never bend down.

This is just asking for trouble. Every child under the age of nine thinks you want to play horsey and will immediately jump on your back.

6. Always have a free hand to defend yourself.

Some fool once said that girls are much gentler than boys. This is a lie. I once made the mistake of picking up Jessica with both hands and going 'Who's Daddy's beautiful little girl?' (or some such nonsense) straight to her face. She giggled with delight and then, realizing that I had left myself open to attack, she got me in the bowling-ball hold. (This is when you stick one finger up your father's nose and curl your thumb behind his upper lip and pull outwards. When his face goes 'poing!' you and your older sister laugh.)

7. Never pretend to be a crocodile.

Little children can never tell the difference between a real crocodile and a pretend one, even when it's just their father lying on the carpet with his mouth open. They will scream, kick you in the teeth and run for their mothers. Then sulk at you for frightening them.

8. Always carry a torch.

Barbie's pink sports car has been known to pick up unsuspecting hitch-hikers at speeds in excess of sixty kilometres an hour across an unlit bedroom. I know this from bitter experience. So, never enter any child's bedroom in the dark without a torch.

9. Never sit down . . .

'Catch me, Daddy!' . . .

    . . . Sorry about that. Where was I?

    Let's try that again.

9. Never sit down suddenly.

Small children love to rearrange things. That's why you find egg whisks in the car console, orange peel under your pillow and plastic pants in the oven. It's also why you find corkscrews hidden in the sofa. I know.

That's why I am typing this standing up.

10. Never let a child put their finger in your mouth.

Unless you want to die of plague.

11. And finally ...

'Catch me, Daddy!'

Excuse me.

'AAAAAAggggHHHH!'

... And finally, most of all, remember,

NEVER TEACH YOUR CHILDREN TO PLAY CATCH ME, DADDY.

I'll have to finish now.

I think the arm's gone again.

CHAPTER 10

Pre-school Tension

The three-year-old itch

Fathers sometimes forget that being three isn't all that easy. Having said that, let's admit that being the father of a three-year-old isn't a great deal easier.

Let me give you an example of what you're going to be up against. It's best to be prepared.

From little biscuits, mighty fights do grow

It all started when I took Jessica with me to a friend's house. She managed to wheedle three ginger nuts and a custard cream out of my friend's wife. I put my foot down when she made a grab for the chocolate crackles. I said she'd make herself sick and that, anyway, she would spoil her tea.

(As if a three-year-old would give a damn about missing broccoli or vomiting over someone else's carpets.)

There was a bit of a scene, so I put her in the car – using the old foot-on-the-chest-while-you-strap-the-buckle method (see 'travelling with children') – and drove home.

We were halfway down the street when Junior unclipped the buckle, wound down the window and tried to clamber out. I slammed on the brakes. As soon as I'd stopped she threw open the door and started hoofing it back up the street. She said she was going back to get her biscuit.

I set off after her. The builders on the site over the road started to applaud. This is the sort of thing that makes a bricklayer's day.

Mind the escalator

By the time we got home I was a little stressed out. I am still nose to nose with my daughter, who refuses to be intimidated.

'When I get to my room I'm going to throw things!' she is yelling at me.

I'm not listening. 'Next time you do that I'll leave you in the street. See if I care if you get run over!'

She climbs on the piano stool so that she can stare me down, eyeball to eyeball. 'I – WANT – ANOTHER – BIS-CUIT!'

'When I say no, I mean no! And if you don't stop crying I'll give you something to cry about!' (Before I had children I swore I'd never ever say that. It's now a standard part of my vocabulary, along with 'Just because, that's why!')

'I WANT ANOTHER BISCUIT!' She runs back to the front door, intending to take off back up the street to our friends' kitchen on a solo commando raid. I lock the door. She unlocks it. I slam it shut. She aims a kick at my shin. I smack her on the bottom.

I think this is what is referred to as 'escalation' on the evening news.

She rushes to her room and slams the door. Then she slams it again. And again. And again.

She has made her point. I now go to make mine. The invasion of Kuwait is replayed in the south wing. It finishes with my announcement: 'And don't bother slamming the door. I'm slamming it!'

SLAM!!

The irresistible father and the immovable child

It is quiet for a while so I venture back, intending to build bridges.

Either the bedroom has been ransacked by the SAS or Jessica has opened all the cupboards and tipped every single thing she possesses on to the floor. She looks up at me with a mixture of defiance and apprehension. 'Nobody loves me.'

'Did you do this?' I hear myself saying.

She looks me straight in the eye and shakes her head. 'A boy did it.'

'Why did you do this?'

'BECAUSE I WANT ANOTHER BISCUIT!'

'Tidy it up this minute!'

She hides under the bed.

'Come out from under there!'

'No! Everyone's shouting at me!'

'When you come out from there I'm going to smack your bottom!'

With laudable commonsense she decides to stay right where she is. She refuses to come out even to get her tea.

The test of a good farver: you get D minus

She's still there at bedtime. 'Come on, Jessie. Time to go to bed!'

'NO!'

I drag her out from hiding, wrestle her into a nightie and put her into bed. 'We've all had enough, all right? It's time to go to bed!'

'I don't want to go to bed! I WANT ANOTHER BISCUIT!'

'You can't have one!'

'But I'm hungry!'

'Well, tea's over. You decided to sulk. That's not our fault! Now go to sleep!'

She plays her trump card. 'You're not a very good farver! You're not very nice!'

Gulp.

So this is fatherhood?

She cried for another hour, complaining bitterly that she was hungry. There wasn't any tea left so my wife gave her a couple of biscuits instead.

When it was over I sat on the sofa and stared in morose silence at the carpet, hating myself for losing control, hating myself for some of the things I had said and done, hating myself because I was a complete failure as a parent. I had no patience and no sense of proportion. I didn't like my three-year-old and I certainly didn't like myself.

The golden rule

Next morning, as usual, Jess bounded into the bedroom, the previous night's live performance of *Nightmare on Elm Street* quite forgotten. She gave me a hug. Her warm tousled hair smelled as fresh as new mown hay.

Then, she and her big sister went to the kitchen and started breakfast. Later that morning, she picked us both flowers. (Okay, she pulled them out of our neighbour's garden by the roots, but she meant well.) We were a family again.

What I had forgotten was that three-year-olds aren't really so terrible. They are angels in disguise. They are loving, giving, innocent, open-hearted and precious.

Just don't ever cross one.

CHAPTER 11

Are We There Yet?

Travelling with children

Once upon a time if you wanted to go somewhere you just jumped in the car and went. Those days are over, my friend. If you plan to go anywhere from now on, you had better be prepared. Children get bored very easily so the key to pleasant travelling with children is to keep them entertained. If you don't put some thought into this, they will play the only game they know: Let's Fight Till The Veins in Dad's Temple Stick Out.

Here are a few suggestions for the sorts of game you might enjoy more:

Old McDonald
Songs are always a good way to entertain the children. 'Row, Row, Row Your Boat', 'Twinkle Twinkle . . . ' and the theme tune from *Neighbours* are all popular but can get a little repetitive if you are going further than, say, your letter box. 'Old McDonald' is better. If you are going on a really long trip – Brighton to Hamburg, for example – you may have to use your imagination and add a few more animals (e.g. 'Old McDonald had a platypus/lesser spotted grebe/combine harvester/butter mountain').

I Spy

I Spy is a great way to pass the time but, after they've done Grass, Tree, Clouds, Sky, Mummy and Cow, it starts to become a little demanding for smaller children and they lose interest. If you try to liven it up and do T for Tachometer, five-year-olds give up and start to cry.

Pre-schoolers, unfettered by knowledge, love this game but are not very good at it. They give clues like 'I Spy with my little eye something beginning with E' when the answer is a cow and you're driving through Birmingham. Older children get upset at this flagrant disregard for the rules and this leads to another popular children's game called:

Bickering

For two or more players. Includes such family favourites as Hair Pulling, Sideways Punching, Snatching, Slapping and Biting. The loser is the one nominated and smacked by the father for 'Starting It'. Game continues until everyone else has been smacked and is therefore 'Out'. The winner is then entitled to poke his tongue out at the others, and the game starts all over again.

The 'I-don't-wanna-go-inna-car game'

A version of Twister. The youngest member of the family is It and starts the game by arching the back and screaming. The object of the game is for one of the parents to strap them in their seat, using whatever means at their disposal. If it's you, the best way is by bracing one leg against the console, and the other on the chest of the one who is It, clicking the buckle with the left hand while holding It's hands with the other hand to prevent them unfastening it again straightaway. Requires practice.

Eating and drinking

A very popular car game. To start, all participants should hide some of their Twisties, bits of Mars bar, biscuits, apple peel and polony sandwiches in the glove box, the crack behind the back seat, under the booster seat, or inside the nodding dog – so Dad can join in the treasure hunt later on.

Players should then eat and drink as much as they possibly can, spill the rest down their front and move on to the next game, which is:

'I need to do wee/poo/sick up'

This is an entertaining and fun game that can liven up even the most boring journey. To start, the player should wait until:

a) The driver is overtaking a lorry in the outside lane of a motorway.
b) The driver is in a traffic jam in the middle of the city.
c) It's raining.
d) Two minutes after they've driven away from McDonald's.

Are we there yet?

This is the best game of them all. The child starts the game by saying 'Are we there yet?' and the father says 'Not yet, dear.' Then the other child says 'How much faaaaa-rther?' and the father says 'Not long now, why don't you just close your eyes and rest?'

At this point the two/three/mob of children in the back will wink at each other, silently count to ten and then the first one says, 'Are we there yet?' and the game starts all over again.

The game is played until the father turns round and screams: *'Will you please shut up and stop nagging. It's miles yet. I wish we'd left you at home!'*

The child who is screamed at is the winner and is then entitled to be It in the next game, which is:

Screaming and crying

Also known as Hysteria (patent pending). For one or more players. Game ends when the driver gives up and takes

everyone home again or turns round to do some screaming himself and stacks the front of the car into the boot of a brand new Mercedes.

Bon voyage!

CHAPTER 12

This Is Going To Hurt You More Than It Hurts Me

Maintaining the illusion of discipline

There was a time, not too long ago, when a father's role was quite simple. He was the family disciplinarian. Children all over the Western world waited in dread 'until their fathers got home', when the day's misdemeanours would be called to account. Disciplining children was simple: all you needed were a few canes, rubber hoses, straps, birches and chains.

Let's not get nostalgic, however.

Childhood was once a violent interlude between searching for scraps on the linoleum kitchen floor and hauling wagons down a coal mine. If you were an intellectual, you earned an hour away from the coal face in order to teach the canary how to say: 'Look out, I'm chok . . . '

Times have changed. Corporal Punishment has given way to General Confusion. No one wants to return to those days of terrible brutality – well, only occasionally – so what do we fathers do, now we are no longer required as torturers and hitmen?

During the peace-love-groovy seventies, a school of thought evolved, which still holds sway in some circles today. Its adherents believed that children should not be disciplined at all; they should be allowed to evolve naturally. Any parental restrictions or interference might permanently damage their little darlings' fragile psyches. This theory was often expounded while the little darling was permanently damaging your fragile record player.

A decade on, you'll have seen the results of their handiwork: rap musicians, coke dealers and computer salesmen.

The Darwinian Peace-Love-Groovy Total-Non-Interference School went back to the repair shop for major overhauls to the shockers. It re-emerged as the Gentle Reasoning Approach.

Let's say some little brat has just grabbed a plate from your kitchen cupboard and thrown it at a playmate. It lies smashed on the floor and the other child has a lump the size of a competition volleyball on his cranium.

The mother approaches the child, stern but concerned. 'Now, why did you do that, Graham?'

'Dunno.'

'Can you see that that was the wrong thing to do?'

'Dunno.'

'I want you to try and articulate your feelings. Now what made you so angry?'

'Dunno.'

'I want you to try and tell me why you felt you had to do that. Do you think that was the right way to resolve the conflict? . . . '

The Gentle Reasoning Approach is a form of psychological torture: not for the child, but for you. The kid can keep saying 'Dunno' all day – it's how most children communicate anyway – but most adults crack after the first five minutes.

'For God's sake, don't keep asking him why he did that! Because he's five years old and he's a little shit, that's why! Here, let him have the Wedgwood to play with!!'

In my experience, there are three reasons why a child misbehaves.

Out of pure ignorance

Attempting to impose any form of discipline on any child who is too young to understand is obviously futile. You cannot ground an eighteen-month-old for tipping custard powder on the floor. He is not going anywhere without you anyway. And appropriate physical measures – garrotting, for example – seem a little unfair when he has no idea of the physical properties of custard powder.

That was why he tipped up the packet.

Until children are old enough to know better (when they're about twenty-seven) you should simply remove them from any situation that is likely to present problems. Stop eating custard. Put all your ornaments on the top shelf. Pack your CD player back in its box and don't listen to music again until after they've left home.

To get attention
Perhaps he feels no one really cares enough about him.
Positive attention is better than negative attention, but
negative attention is better than none at all. In other words
a child would rather be abhorred than ignored. You have to
ensure that your children do get enough of your time, and
your love. They crave your approval. The corollary to this,
however, is that they have to feel your approval is worth
having. Which leads to the third point:

Sheer bastardy
They want to test your mettle. It's a way of finding out if
you're all mouth and trousers. Girls are all little Thatchers
looking for a Wet. Boys are all Saddams looking for a
Kuwait.

Be warned.
    Know your limits. Make them liberal and reasonable, but
make them inviolable.
    Heard this song before?
    'If you don't stop that I'm going to lose my temper in a
minute . . . I'm telling you one last time . . . Look, I'm not
telling you again . . . How many times have I told you . . .
I've told you this before . . . If I have to lose my temper
with you . . . '
    That does not work. When your kindly nature is abused,
this does:
    Count to three aloud. If the behaviour isn't corrected,
you get up and you enforce your rules without hesitation.
Now, physical intimidation is not what I'm advocating here
(although I have found a blowtorch and a Bowie knife
work particularly well with two of my nephews). Different
motivators work for different children. What works best?
A gentle tap on the tail? Being sent to their room for five
minutes' time out? But if you have an ace to play, play it.
As the saying goes, you can do anything with a bayonet
except sit on it.

Make no mistake, what we are talking about here is survival. *Your* survival. As a sane, functioning, rational human being. And don't get hooked into a moral debate.

'Aw, dad, why do I have to stop pouring paint stripper on next door's car?'

Don't say: 'Because it's naughty' or 'Because Mr Jones will get cross.' One is subjective opinion, the other is sheer speculation. They just invite debate.

The answer should be: 'BECAUSE I DON'T WANT YOU TO.'

Try practising this a few times. There. Doesn't that feel better?

The golden rule is this: Speak Loudly and Carry a Large Carrot and a Small Stick. You sometimes see parents fly into a rage and tell their children they are going to behead them with meat cleavers and hang their headless bodies off the pergola for the sparrows to nibble at on cold mornings. Half the time, they fail to make good on their threats.

Don't make the same mistake. Threatening an early bedtime and meaning it is far more effective than continual warnings of a dire thrashing. Don't forget – children invented brinkmanship. Testing you out is like riding a motorbike at a hundred miles an hour. The danger makes it fun.

More is less. Children are, after all, just small people. They respond best to love, approval, appreciation, bribes and occasional offers of Mars bars.

Having said that, don't forget: rules are made to be broken. Or, more correctly, you cannot invent rules for every conceivable situation. Sometimes you will find yourself drawn into a war that you had no reason to fight. In parenting, as in politics, remember Vietnam.

Which leads me to the last golden rule, and the Great Gumnut Disco Debacle.

On the night of this particular event – Lauren's first disco – we anticipated problems. Hairdressing for Lauren, Lauren's friend and little Jessica had already occupied the better part of Helen's afternoon. Now, she lay on the sofa, eyes glassy from two hours of crimping, curling, tressing and ribbon-tying.

Meanwhile, I found Lauren in her bedroom, wearing long socks and shiny shoes and nothing else, staring into her clothes cupboard.

'What's the matter, honey?'

'I'm sick of my wardrobe. I just don't have a thing to wear!'

'You've got lots of clothes.'

'Everyone's seen everything I've got!'

'There must be something you'd like to wear.'

'My red dress and my blue bloomers.'

'Well, wear them then.'

'Can I? Oh, goody!'

A few moments later, there are voices raised in the laundry. When I arrive I quickly take in the situation and realize I have been suckered in. Again.

'But you wore your red dress at Ruth's birthday party last night,' Helen is explaining. 'It's got tomato sauce all over the front. And your bloomers are still on the line. They're wet.'

'But Daddy said I could wear them!'

'Your father doesn't know what he's talking about,' Helen says, perhaps not unreasonably.

'There must be something else you can wear,' I say, helpfully.

'But there just isn't,' Lauren sobs, and rushes out. She throws herself on her bed, devastated. Her little white shoulders heave with despair. Her life might as well be over. What's the point of going on if she can't wear her blue bloomers?

It is twenty to seven. The disco started ten minutes ago.

'Look Lauren, if you don't hurry up you're going to miss the disco.'

'You said I could wear my red dress and my blue bloomers!'

'I didn't know they were in the wash.'

'You lied to me!' Heave, sob.

Time to change tactics. Enough of James Baker, time to give her some Norman Schwarzkopf. 'Look, young lady, your little sister and Ruth are all ready to go! If you don't get off that bed and get dressed this minute we're going without you!'

'I don't care!'

'Right. That's it then.' Never make idle threats, isn't that what I said?

I turn around and see Helen staring at me the way you might stare at a small child trying to make a square block fit into a circular hole by hitting it with a hammer. 'This isn't going to work,' she mutters.

'EVERYONE JUST GET IN THE CAR!'

The kids pile in the car. I slam the front door. I slam the car door. I start the engine and rev it. By now Lauren must have got the point. I start to reverse out of the driveway.

The door opens and Lauren appears.

'See,' I say to Helen.

Lauren is still naked except for shoes and socks. Her face is screwed up with despair. She waves a pathetic goodbye to us and the door closes again.

I know when I'm beaten. I mean, what I am trying to prove? I'm thirty-eight, for God's sake. I'm behaving like a child. Is it really so important what she wears? 'How wet are the bloomers, Helen?'

'Well, damp – not really wet.'

'And I guess with a red dress you can't really notice tomato sauce stains.'

'No, not really.'

Ten minutes later, Lauren is at the Gumnut Disco doing the Birdie dance in a stained red dress and damp blue bloomers. She looks as if she has been dressed with a shovel but she is ecstatically happy. Which proves my final rule about parenting, one that may not please the experts or the theorists but they don't have to live with Lauren. The last golden rule is this:

When in doubt – *give in!*

CHAPTER 13

The Blood of Others

Can friendship survive children?

Fatherhood will change many things for you. It will change your relationship with your wife, it will change the way you think about yourself, and it will change the way you see life. It will also change the way you look at your friends.

A great friendship can survive many things: misunderstanding, thoughtlessness, distance, fire and rain. But can it survive children?

Bette Midler: you gotta have friends

Take Simon and Jessica for instance. We had a longstanding friendship with Simon's parents: I got on well with him, my wife got on well with her, we both had children who sat next to each other in grade one.

It was our Jessica and their Simon that was the problem.

I don't care what anybody says: boys and girls are different from day one. Girls like Care Bears and dressing up and drawing and *My Favourite Pony* and playing Mums and Dads and using their mother's lipstick and holding other people's babies. Boys like shouting 'Cowabunga!'

and smashing heads off things with sticks.

Now, I don't deny that there may come a day when Jessica and Simon will look at each other across a crowded room and there will be violins and fireworks and hearts beating as one. But, for now, the genetic differences that may make for moons in June later on are just a catalyst for the sort of unspeakable violence you normally only witness on the evening news.

Suffer little children

So when Jessica looked up from her Rainbow Brite puzzle and saw Simon and his mother walking up the drive, her reaction was immediate. She screamed 'GO AWAY!', slammed the front door and locked it. When my wife opened it again, she howled in anguish and ran down the hallway to the bedroom and started hiding the remains of her headless Barbie dolls.

On this particular day, Simon had been transformed into Donatello, a Ninja Turtle. Some lunatic had given him a mask and a plastic sword. Where there is suffering, he will add to it; where there is injustice, he will do his best to make it a lot worse; where there is evil, he will make *Nightmare on Elm Street* look like the Teddy Bears Picnic.

While the respective mothers shot up on some badly needed caffeine, Jessica and the Hero in a Half Shell were ordered to play nicely and share, even though this seems to me blatantly impossible. Asking a three-year-old to share is like asking Colonel Gaddafi to salute the Stars and Stripes.

From the study, I listened while the Battle of Leningrad was replayed downstairs. There were wails and screams and cries of anguish interspersed with occasional ceasefires to tend the wounded.

From your lips to God's ear

I tried to tune it out. After all, I was supposed to be working. This was really none of my business.

But I couldn't help thinking that my daughter seemed to be getting the worst of it. My paternal protective urges began to force themselves to the surface. A pencil snapped in half between my fingers. Then another. And another . . .

At last, I heard the patter of tiny feet on the stairs. Jessica appeared, tears glistening on her cheeks like tiny dewdrops. 'Dad . . . '

'What's the matter, honey?'

'Simon fumped me.'

'Did he?' I resist an insane urge to go and throttle the brat who did this to my little girl. I hear myself saying: 'Well . . . you thump him back.'

Sniffle. 'But Mummy said not to fump anyone.'

'No, you mustn't. But it's different if he thumps you first.'

'But Mummy says I mustn't . . . '

'Well, Daddy says you can.'

She immediately brightened. This was more like it. She looked at me the way I imagine George Bush looked when the United Nations gave him approval to use force to impose sanctions against Iraq. 'Okay,' she said, and dashed back down the stairs.

A few moments later, I heard her announce in a loud voice: 'Daddy told me to fix Simon.'

Reliable witnesses tell me that it was at this point that she picked up her dolls' house and dropped it on Simon's head, thus bringing the Siege of Leningrad, morning coffee and a longstanding friendship to an abrupt and hysterical end.

Another one bites the dust

I watched from the study as mother helped a slightly groggy Ninja Turtle stagger home, one hand (flipper?) still clutching his head, his screams echoing down the street until they were out of sight.

Uh-oh.

'Congratulations,' my wife says to me, from the top of the stairs.

'I suppose you're going to blame me for that.'

'Did you tell her to go and hit Simon with the dolls' house?'

'I'm being quoted out of context.'

'Well, thanks for all your help.'

And that was that. The result of it all was that Simon's mother was no longer talking to my wife. Simon was not talking to Jessica. (Suited her fine.) My wife was not talking to me. In fact, nobody was talking to me, including Simon's father and Jessica (who had sided with the majority – there's loyalty for you).

Maybe things will improve, come puberty.

Sigh.

Ah well. Who needs friends? After all, you have your children to care for you in the loneliness of your old age.

Points to remember:

1 Boys and girls go together like nitrogen and glycerine.
2 If you make a mistake, try not to blame yourself. There will be plenty of others who will do it for you.
3 Never allow anyone to quote you, least of all reporters and children.
4 Don't make friends with anyone who already has children. Such people are basically unstable.
5 Never interfere. Let the women sort it out. Then stand back and criticize.

Questions to think about:

- Did you spot my deliberate mistake?
- Why didn't I?
- Should they bring back the death penalty in kindergarten? yes ☐ no ☐
- After all, what are friends for? Illustrate your answer with diagrams.

CHAPTER 14

The Watergate Effect

The hazards of answering questions

One of the hardest things about being a father is answering your children's questions. If you're a modern father, you'll subscribe to the glasnost theory, which advocates openness and honesty at all times, with the attendant hazards.

Do you have clear and precisely-formed opinions on sex and mortality? No? Better hurry up and get some.

Heaven's above! Or is it?

One day, my girls saw a squirrel hanging from the power lines at the end of the street. It had been electrocuted. Lauren and Jess both have a glove puppet called Mister Nutty who has a passing resemblance to a squirrel so, naturally, they were mortified.

'What's wrong with it?' Lauren asked me.

'It's dead,' I told her.

'What's dead?'

'Well, it's when . . . it's sort of gone to sleep . . . It's like when you pick a flower and it wilts and then . . . Well, it depends which religion you believe and . . . '

She frowned and put her hands on her hips. 'Look, if you don't know, say so. I'll ask my teacher.'

It depends on whether the squirrel was a Buddhist

Death is a tough one. Has the squirrel been re-incarnated as another squirrel, or perhaps as a higher form of life, like a hedgehog? Or has it passed on to a better life in squirrel heaven, where all the power lines are underground? Or is it just well . . . dead? And what about Mister Nutty, the glove puppet? He can't move unless I stick my hand up his back . . . so is he dead? If he is . . . shouldn't we bury him?

Sex is much easier than death. There are no imponderables. You just answer the questions as they come up. It's simply a matter of being open.

Our family practised its own form of glasnost long before it became fashionable. However, as President Gorbachev discovered, openness can lead to anarchy and confusion, even with something as simple as sex instruction.

Do they have sex in Northampton?

One day, when Lauren was five, she asked us where she came from.

We sat her down and told her the whole story, then we got out a book and showed her some pictures, trying to keep our explanations interesting but thorough, simple but not unnervingly so.

She endured it all with an expression of increasing boredom, if not hostility. Finally she blurted out: 'Yes, but where did I come from?'

'But we just told you,' I said.

She stamped her foot, as if we were deliberately trying to frustrate her. 'Rachel's from Northampton. Where am I from?'

'Oh, well . . . you were born in London,' Helen said.

Exit one child, muttering. We heard her run off down the verandah steps with Rachel.

'So where are you from?' we heard Rachel ask.

'They don't seem sure,' Lauren answered. 'I think they're getting old. You know, like Doctor Coldheart in the Care Bears.'

Glasnost for tots

In fact, Lauren does not seem all that interested in sex, or else she already knows all about it, I'm not sure which. Although I don't doubt I'll find out one of these days. On the other hand, by the time Jessica was two years old she was obsessively interested.

Having learned our lesson with her older sister, we tried to answer all her questions as succinctly as possible. This approach also leads to problems, however. The other day, my wife was walking round the supermarket with Jess sitting in the front of the trolley. She leaned out, tapped a complete stranger on the arm, pointed to my wife with her finger and said to him: 'They're my Mum's boobs!'

I believe he congratulated her and walked quickly on.

Glasnost extends to the bathroom. The door is never locked. The children know they can wander in and out as they like; Lauren always enjoyed taking showers with me when the mood took her, and I offered this option to Jessica.

One day, I was getting into the shower when the girls walked in looking for a particular bath toy. Jess stopped and stared at me as if I was deformed.

'What's that?' she said, pointing.

So I told her.

'Will I have a penis when I'm a big girl?' she asked.

Lauren looked at her, exasperated. 'Don't be silly! You won't look like that when you're big. You'll look normal – like Mummy.'

Thanks, kids. In future, I'll lock the door.

Well, your mother doesn't seem to mind it

But of course it doesn't end there. With children nothing is ever finished with. It's like a virus in a computer. You never know when something you've programmed in will pop up again and ruin your day.

Which is what happened a week later when one of my wife's friends came round. Helen was out, picking Lauren up from school.

'She'll only be five minutes,' I told her. 'Want a cup of coffee?'

She said yes, she'd love one. Jess, always looking for a new friend to ingratiate herself with, plonked herself on her lap and showed her her new Barbie doll.

As I was bringing the coffees from the kitchen, Jess

pointed to me and said, in a stage-whisper, 'My Daddy's got a penis!' And, she added: 'It's *yuk*!'

I decided at about this time that glasnost might be over. But once you've started, it's too late to stop. Once you let the bourgeoisie have their way, there's no turning back. So much for glasnost.

And I still haven't figured out what happens to squirrels when they die.

Points to remember:

1 Children can deal with the intricacies of sex and death better than you can.
2 Answer one question at a time. Sex instruction should take place over five years, not five minutes.
3 Never say: 'You'll look like this one day.' A child may never get over the trauma.
4 Always try and answer as truthfully as you can.
5 While doing this, try not to sound like a dork.

Questions to think about:

• Why do things die? Answer in ten words or less. Do not use words of more than two syllables.
• Explain sexual reproduction. Do not refer to rabbits or the Baby Jesus or storks.
• What is God? (More paper is available at the front desk.)
• What happens to squirrels when they die?

CHAPTER 15

If Pain Persists

What's up, doc?

There are two places where children really feel at home. One is in a playground, the other is in a doctor's surgery.

Let me give you a tip. Once your children are born, buy yourself a season ticket at the local surgery; get your wife to make a firm booking for, say, every Wednesday at 5 p.m.. Then she only has to ring up if she doesn't need to go. You'll save more money on phone calls that way.

Let's look at how it works:

WEEK 1

Case History: Lauren had us worried. She had been prone to occasional bouts of asthma since eighteen months, and now she seemed wheezy, had a bad cough, and had blown a low 120 on her peak flow metre. When she's healthy, she normally blows 175.

Treatment: Off to the surgery for our weekly 5 p.m. consultation. Doctor Mike smiled at her and asked her to blow as hard as she could into the flow metre for him.

She responded to his silken charm with a 225, an all-time record.

'How come you blow 125 for us, and 225 for him?' I asked her when we got into the car afterwards.

'You don't give me a jelly bean,' she said.

WEEK 2

Case History: A bad case of MTH (My Tummy Hurts!) combined with a runny nose. 'Not much we can do. I think it's just a virus,' I said.

'We'd better get it checked out,' Helen said.

Treatment: Off to see Doctor Mike for the regular booking.

'I think it's a virus,' he said. 'Not much we can do.'

WEEK 3

Case History: The runny nose is gone, but Lauren still has the MTH, combined with a bad attack of MBI (My Bottom Itches!).

Treatment: Doctor Mike is reassuring.

'Just worms,' he says. 'They're very common, especially in primary school children. If you go in the bedroom at night you'll see them.'

'You mean – like glow worms?'

'Well, you'll need a torch.'

'Sounds fun.'

He wrote out a prescription. 'Here. Just one dose should do it. It doesn't taste too bad. You can get it in banana flavour.'

'Hear that, Lauren? It doesn't taste too bad.'

'Not just Lauren. You'll all have to take it.'

'All of us?'

'You'll have to be de-wormed as a precaution.' He passed

me a jelly bean with a pair of forceps. 'See you next week.
Don't touch anything on the way out.'

Later that night my wife sprang out of bed and bounded
into the girls' room. I opened one eye and saw torchlight
flickering on the wall.

'Look, Col! I can see them!'

See what? I wondered sleepily. Stars? Comets? Little
green men in the garden?

I stumbled out of bed and across the hallway. Helen
was shining a torch under Lauren's bedclothes. 'Look,'
she whispered, 'Mike was right! They do come out at
night! See!'

Or maybe it was just a nightmare I had.

WEEK 4

Case History: The banana juice has done its work and got
rid of the glow worms. Lauren is over the the MBI but still
has the MTH. Wednesday at 1700 hours we are back at
Doctor Mike's.

Treatment: 'We'll run some tests,' he says. 'I'll have to
examine her stool.'

'Which one?' I ask innocently, wondering what on earth
her baby furniture had to do with it. 'The red plastic one,
or the nice pine one her grandad made for her?'

He gives me a pitying look and hands my wife a small
plastic specimen bottle. 'In there,' he says.

The next twenty-four hours were spent clutching the
specimen jar, waiting for our daughter to announce the
Big Event. When it came, I rushed to get my scuba mask
and snorkel. Lauren took one look at me and locked the
toilet door.

My wife snatched the specimen jar away. 'Here,' she said
wearily, 'take that damn thing off. I'll do it.'

After much grunting and groaning on the other side of the door – from all concerned – the treasure was rushed to the doctor's surgery, sirens blaring. Unfortunately, the tests came back negative. We were back where we started.

'Could be a virus,' Doctor Mike suggested.

WEEK 5

Case History: Lauren still has her MTH, so we start making an inventory of her diet. Perhaps it's an allergy? But then medical science achieves the breakthrough we have been praying for. As Lauren is getting into the bath my wife notices a red mark around her middle.

'Is the elastic on your school uniform too tight?' she asks.

She nods eagerly: 'Yeah.'

'Do you think that that's why your tummy has been hurting?'

'Yeah!' she says brightly, as if she had been wondering why it had taken us so long to figure it out.

Treatment: Loosen the elastic on the school uniform. Ring Doctor Mike and cancel the appointment. Endure snivelling on the other end of the line as he wonders aloud how he's going to pay the lease on his Saab this month.

WEEK 6

Case History: Lauren is in peak physical condition but Jessica looks pale. She has an MTH with a possible MBI and a triple U (Unspecified and Undefinable Unwellness).

Treatment: Back to Doctor Mike's. Try not to dent his Saab as you park your Honda Civic.

Points to remember:

1 Don't try and kill worms with a torch and a hammer.
2 There is always something you can do about a virus. You can go to the doctor's who can then tell you there is nothing you can do.
3 Never stand on a stool.
4 An MTH could be a ETT (Elastic Too Tight).
5 If pain persists, see your doctor.

CHAPTER 16

What's Wrong Now?

Kids' illnesses – what your family doctor never told you

Most fathers worry endlessly about their children, especially when they get sick: worry a bit too much, in fact. Normal, healthy kids are sick a lot. If they don't get sick, there's something wrong with them.

To allay some of those father's fears, the following is a guide to a selection of the more common ailments and what to do about them, including a lot of things your family doctor never told you.

Broken bones

This is quite a common ailment in parents who have been struck with a butterfly ball in a fight over eating up all the peas. Broken fingers and wrists often occur after making desperate lunges on hearing the magic words: 'Catch me!'

Since it is impossible to function properly as a father while in plaster, take an aspirin, keep the affected part as immobile as possible and see a doctor as soon as the child starts school.

Child-battering

Child-battering is a serious and little discussed problem. Children between the ages of two and three can be extremely violent and are liable to scratch, bite and punch at the slightest provocation, especially when crossed. If you feel you are in danger of becoming child-battered, you should:

a) Never turn your back on them for a moment.
b) Never bend down if the child appears to be angry.
c) Give in to them whenever practical.
d) See your doctor if pain persists.

Colic

Also known as chronic crying. Doctors call it colic because it tends to offer a pathetic ray of hope to parents who might otherwise contemplate suicide. There is no known cure for colic except lifelong chastity.

No, not for the baby: for *you*!

Deafness

Deafness in children is an extremely common problem. It is usually brought on by being asked to do something they don't want to do (e.g. tidy their room). You should only see your doctor if the child has obvious hearing problems: if they cannot hear a chocolate bar being unwrapped through two closed doors at a distance of one hundred metres, for example.

Diarrhoea

Childhood diarrhoea can easily be avoided. It is usually brought on when the child knows they have you at their mercy and there's nothing you can do about it. To prevent diarrhoea:

a) Never take them on a bus.
b) Never dress them in white.
d) Don't get them christened.
e) Never put them in a friend's swimming pool.

Elastoplastitis

Elastoplastitis is a recent medical phenomenon. Since all children are chronically addicted to sympathy, they can often say the word Elastoplast before they can sit upright, and demand one for everything from a snagged toenail to a sore haircut. In chronic cases, children become so dependent on Elastoplasts that they suffer severe vitamin D starvation due to sunlight being unable to penetrate through to their skin. Use sparingly. No more than fifty on one child at any time.

Head banging

Rhythmically knocking the head against something hard –

a wall, or a door – is a common enough problem, most often found in parents who have been

a) Trying to teach a child to share.
b) Or trying to persuade a two-year-old to eat broccoli.

Hyperventilation

A common childhood problem resulting in vertigo, light-headedness, spots before the eyes and fainting. Usually found in adults at birthday parties after blowing up too many balloons.

Masturbation

This is not an illness, although some parents treat it as if it is. Masturbation is definitely not something to worry about. (Just think how much it saves you on expensive toys.) Children are naturally curious, and although the habit may be socially embarrassing, most girls grow out of it by the time they are four or five. Boys may take a little longer: eighty-four or eighty-five.

Nightmares

Many children have nightmares. It's no good screaming: 'It's three in the morning! How can there be a Big Purple Crocodile under a trundle bed on the seventh floor of a security apartment block?'

Children tend to be irrational and you will have to go along with it. Get an axe or meat tenderizer and get under the child's bed and simulate a fight to the death with the Big Purple Crocodile. Make plenty of noise: and don't fall asleep under there or the child will assume the Big Purple Crocodile has eaten you and scream even louder.

Pretend to drag the body of the Big Purple Crocodile from the room, wrapped in a bunny rug. Kiss the child goodnight and go back to bed. Make sure the Big Purple Crocodile is dead, or it may come after you for revenge later.

Pain

Don't panic if the child comes to you screaming. Calmly ask the child what hurts, and why. Children tend to be a little over-dramatic at times. Stepping on a thorn can send them into convulsions and a broken toenail can bring on total collapse: all this from a child who will pull out its own front teeth to get twenty pence from the tooth fairy two weeks early. The best known analgesic is an Elastoplast and a biscuit.

Plague

A much under-rated problem. Plague can be carried by bath toys, the corpses of small animals secreted in matchboxes under the child's pillow or from picking up a baby with severe cradle cap. For some reason, children are totally immune but there is a significant risk to parents. You should never allow a child to put their fingers in your mouth. If this happens, seek medical advice immediately.

Poisoning

While it is vital to keep household chemicals, garden poisons and prescription drugs well out of a child's reach, you should not worry too greatly over some of the more common substances. Children as young as eighteen months have been known to eat a whole pack of Kleenex, including the box, without any apparent side-effects.

It has been calculated that, on average, most children eat a kilo of sand by the time they are three years old. Apart from the abrasive effect (if you find your child's nappy in shreds in the morning, keep them away from the sandpit for a few days) it is apparently harmless. Children have remarkably strong constitutions. The only thing known to make them gag is fresh celery.

Rigidity

Many children suffer from this condition, also known as toddler mortis. The only known cure is to let the child have its own way.

Sleeping

All children suffer from sleeping problems at some stage – and so a routine is vital. At the same time every night you should tuck them in, read them a story, sing them a song, turn off the lights, leave the room, shout threats through the door, get them a drink, shout more threats, let them get up to go to the toilet, tell them you won't tell them again, get them medicine for their stomach ache, tell them you won't tell them again, sit with them because they're frightened of the dark, go out, shout threats, tell them you won't tell them again, sing them another song, tell them it's absolutely the last time, then sit with them until they fall asleep.

Deviate from this routine and you could find yourself with a child with sleeping problems.

Sniffing

All children sniff. This is not, as some doctors believe, because of allergic rhinitis or similar complaints, but because they like to hear you say 'stop sniffing'.

No known cure.

Vomiting

There are many reasons for children vomiting but it is usually brought on by picking up a child when wearing your best clothes e.g. just as you're about to go out to dinner.

Try not to go out to dinner. Enjoying yourself is for singles.

CHAPTER 17

Saying Goodbye to Guinea

An adult discussion about heavy petting: how far should they go?

The first word our girls learned to say was 'no'. The second word was 'mum'. The third thing they learned to say was: 'Can I have a pet?'

I vowed we would never have any pets when I learned a salutary lesson from some neighbours we once had. They started off in a small way, buying a goldfish for their five-year-old daughter. Then her three-year-old brother saw dad catching fish down the beach and decided to try it for himself. He filleted the goldfish for that night's tea.

To comfort the distraught daughter, they bought her a budgie. Two days later, it fell off the perch – so to speak.

To soften this second blow, they bought her a parrot. But to prove he was no pretty boy, he put his beak through her thumbnail. So they bought her a rabbit instead.

They woke up one morning and found the rabbit (the pet shop owner had told them it was a male) nursing a litter of twenty little bundles of fluff. They figured:

a) He was not a male and was pregnant when they bought him.
b) He was a male but had won custody.
c) He had reproduced parthogenetically, like an amoeba.
d) The parrot was responsible.

The girl's little brother grew attached to one with a black patch over its right eye. It was the only one of all twenty to die.

They bought him a puppy to console him. He called him Flowerpot. One day, a visiting uncle took Flowerpot for a walk down the beach. He ran off and the uncle couldn't bring himself to yell 'Flowerpot!' on a crowded beach so he came back without him. They never saw him again.

The little boy was disconsolate for a week so they decided to buy him yet another pet to take his mind off the loss. By the time we left the area they had two axolotls, three hamsters, a Weimaraner, two Burmese, two budgerigars, a Mynah bird and a seagull with a broken wing that they were teaching to talk. It could say: 'Throw us another chip, sport!'

Not us, we vowed. No pets in our house.

Meet guinea and pig

But we reckoned without the intense psychological pressure two young daughters can bring to bear. We finally relented and bought them both a guinea pig. What harm could it do?

'He's cute!' Jessica shouted when she saw hers. He was too. A little white thing, like an elongated mouse. The other one was brown. Fortunately, they make guinea pigs in different colours so you can tell them apart.

'What will you call him?' I asked her.

'Guinea,' she said.

'What about yours?' I asked Lauren.

She thought about this for a moment. 'Pig,' she said.

And kids are supposed to have unfettered imaginations.

You've got it, or you ain't

Guinea won hearts immediately. Jess carried him round all day, like a baby. She didn't even mind when he peed on her.

Lauren ignored hers and whined that she wanted to have a turn of Jessica's, which is typical. Even my wife joined in.

'Here, let me have a hold.'

'No,' Jess said. 'He's mine!'

'Let me have a hold or you can go to your room!'

Really. A grown woman.

Ou sont les guinea pigs d'antan?

That night, we tucked Guinea and Pig up in their straw, made sure they had plenty of lettuce, carrot and apple, refilled their dish with cavie food, examined their water dispenser for microbes, covered them up, all had a turn at wishing them goodnight, and went to sleep.

Next morning, Guinea was dead.

Now don't ask me why. Maybe he fell off the little stairs that led to the penthouse suite in his cage. Maybe he ate too much cavie food. Maybe he just did it to spite me.

Whatever the reason, I rushed to intercept the girls on their way through the laundry to the verandah. 'Er . . . uh . . . I wouldn't go out there if I were you.'

'I want to play with Guinea!' Jess shouted.

'He's er . . . um . . . gone to Guinea Pig Heaven.'

Lauren looked at me as if I'd gone crazy. 'You mean he's dead?'

Jessica's smile fell away. 'Did the police shoot him?'

Obviously been watching too many cop shows. 'No, darling, the police didn't shoot him. He's just . . . well, he was getting old and . . . '

'You said he was only a month old,' Lauren said.

Smart arse. 'Well, that's a long time for guinea pigs.'

'No, it's not. They live till they're five.'

That's the trouble with teaching kids to read.

The plot thickens

A little while later, we gather round a little plot I have prepared under the apple tree. Despite all this crap about equal parenting, you'll still find it's the father that is supposed to bury all the decomposed corpses and despatch the goldfish down the toilet bowl. Be warned.

Jess is holding Guinea in both hands. 'He's not dead!' she shouted. 'His eyes are open!'

'Things can still be dead, darling, even if their eyes are open.'

She looked at her sister, then her mother, then at me. 'Are we dead?'

'No, darling. Our legs aren't sticking up in the air.'

I persuaded her to put Guinea in the little hole. 'Goodbye Guinea,' she whispered, and then her face crumpled with grief. Lauren started to howl then. So did Helen.

Oh, for goodness sake.

I barely have time to erect the cross under the apple tree . . .

Guinea
Gone but not misplaced

2.5.91–3.5.91

. . . before we are piling back in the car and headed for the pet shop. The girls need something to take their mind off their loss.

So does Helen.

That was a month ago. Anyone want to buy a rabbit? What about a kitten? Or there's two Weimaraner puppies going cheap . . .

A FATHER'S QUICK AND EASY REFERENCE GUIDE TO PETS

GOLDFISH

Do not need to be taken for walks, will not dig up the garden or get scales on the furniture in the lounge. On the downside, though, they are extremely boring after the first three minutes and tend not to live much longer than that anyway. Take care when flushing corpses down the toilet. Anything larger than

a guppy (a Mexican walking fish or a fully grown carp, for example) may block the pipes.

BUDGERIGARS

Not as fragile as goldfish, although only marginally less boring. They can even learn to talk, though their conversation tends never to make any more sense than listening to Janet Street Porter. The big downside with budgies is that they invariably escape through open windows and get themselves eaten by the neighbour's Burmese cat. You then have an inconsolable child and a laundry cupboard full of millet on your hands.

RABBITS

Rabbits are cute, fluffy, reasonably easy and cheap to feed, and do not need to be taken for a hop around the block. However, they are worse than sixteen-year-old girls for getting themselves pregnant, even when locked up on their own twenty-four hours a day. Every few weeks, you have a dozen little rabbits to find a home for.

It has been suggested that this problem may be overcome with the aid of a sharp knife, an oven and a few roast potatoes. This method is not recommended for those who would like to be remembered fondly by their children in later years.

DOGS

Dogs are faithful, fun, usually protective of children, and can even be excellent guards. On the downside, they will poop on the floor, dig holes in the garden, bark all night and leave fur all over the cushions. Children will swear to you cross-their-heart that if you will buy them one they will feed it and take it for walks but this is what is known as a politician's promise. It only lasts a week.

Remember too, that if you buy a Weimaraner or a Saint Bernard as a cute little puppy that it will grow into a monster the size of a Shetland pony and will consume the equivalent of ten racehorses every day. Smaller dogs will yap and chew anything not made of stainless steel.

CATS

Teenage girls adore cats. Like teenage girls they are vain, self-obsessed and lazy. Smaller children also adore them and follow them around pulling on their flea collars and tugging on their tails until the animal turns around and rakes them with its claws. They will then ignore it for three minutes.

For adult males, cats do not have an upside. They murder defenceless birds, wee on the carpets, bring fleas into the house, eat the fish you caught and left in the refrigerator, leave fur balls on the furniture, poop on your side of the bed, and generally stink up the house.

Try to avoid buying your children a cat under all circumstances. Consider ferrets and rats first.

HAMSTERS AND GUINEA PIGS

Hamsters and guinea pigs are small, furry and cute. Small children adore them. On the down side, they have a tendency to die of fright if a door slams in a house two doors down, and also tend to carry ringworm.

They pass pellets not poop, so they are not too offensive around the house.

HORSES

Almost every child would love a horse. However, they are not recommended for the home, or the average backyard. They are incredibly expensive to feed and maintain, so should only be considered if you have a farm, or are very rich, like a drug baron, a master criminal or a solicitor.

CHAPTER 18

The Umpire is a Jerk

When not to interfere

As a parent I've made my fair share of mistakes. One of the biggest came when, somewhere along the line, I bought the idea that a father's main responsibility is to referee his children's fights.

Let me paint the picture for you. You are sitting down reading a book or listening to Sinead O'Connor and pretending you are a real human being. You are interrupted by screams from what is jocularly known around here as the family room. War room, more like. Finally, Lauren appears, clutching her side.

'What's wrong?'

'Jessie did it!'

Jessica puts her hands on her hips. 'Did NOT!'

'Did so!'

'Girls, girls. Stop it. All right, Lauren, you first. What happened?'

'Jessie started it.'

Did NOT, Jess mouths silently behind her back.

'What did she do?'

'She bit me.' Did too. There is a livid bruise, fitting established dental records of my youngest daughter, on Lauren's hip.

Fireworks. 'Did you bite her, young lady? I told you never ever to bite!'

Jessica takes a step backwards in the face of her father's righteous wrath. She screws up her face and a fat tear rolls down her cheek. 'But she was sitting on my tummy!'

'Well, you don't have to bite her! Just tell her to get off!'

'I did. She wouldn't.'

'Lauren, why didn't you get off her when she asked you to?'

'I didn't hear her,' she says. And then, so help me, poker-faced, 'How did I know she didn't want me to sit on her stomach?'

Parental cool, feeble thing that it is anyway, is blown at this point. 'Well, if you sit on people's stomachs, expect to get bitten!'

Lauren bursts into tears and throws herself on her bed.

Jessica is far from impressed with the referee's decision, even though it has gone in her favour. 'Oh, Daddy,' she growls at me, 'you made my sister cwy!'

'Let her cry if she wants to,' I say, as I make my exit.

'Big bully!' she yells after me and slams the door.

The professional foul

Well done, ump. Really solved that one, didn't you?

But do you think the old man has learned his lesson? No way. Wait for another foul to get called and here he comes running.

'Now what?'

'Jessie pulled my hair!'

'Did NOT!'

Lauren turns round and pulls Jessica's hair. Jess screams and launches a haymaker in retaliation. It would have gone to a points decision but the referee intervened.

'Look, why are you two hitting each other?'

I get chapter and verse. 'I was playing with the special Barbie doll and Jessie came and took it off me and she wouldn't give it back.'

'Did NOT!'

'Shhh! Look, you two have got nine Barbie dolls and six Kens and two pink Barbie Ferraris, for goodness sake. Why fight over one doll?'

'It's special.'

I can't see what's so special about it. They all look like anorexic Samantha Foxes to me. I utter the immortal cry of the desperate father: 'Why can't you two share?'

'I had it first,' Lauren says.

'Did NOT!'

I blow the whistle again. 'Fine. Okay. If you can't share, you won't have it at all. *I'll* have it. Consider it confiscated.'

Neither of them knows what 'confiscated' means but they howl in anguish anyway. My wife enters. 'What's going on?'

'Daddy took our favourite doll away,' Jessica sobs.

'Did not,' I hear myself say.

'For goodness sake, Colin, they're both over-tired, that's all.'

'That's no excuse.'

'Put on a video or something.'

'Look, I'm sorting this out, okay? I never interfere when you . . . ' And so on.

Well, you know what happens next. Helen and I have a stand-up fight. When we finish chewing bits off each other, we look around and find the girls playing happily on the floor. With the Barbie dolls.

That's two penalty points, Mister McEnroe

Finally, I wised up. It took me long enough, but I got there in the end. One morning, as usual, they shot out the front door and raced for the car, both wanting to be 'first'. Then they exchanged blows over who should open the car door first. Okay, you and I know there are three other doors on the average family saloon, but they both wanted to open the same one. Once inside, they tore into each other over who was going to sit in the middle.

God give me strength.

I put my head through the window and smiled at them. 'I'm going back inside to have another cup of coffee with your mother. Tell me when you're finished. Two falls or a knockdown decides it.'

When I returned they were both strapped in. Lauren was in the coveted middle seat. 'We sorted it out for ourselves,' she announced. 'I'll sit here on the way to school, Jessica will sit here on the way home.'

'Well done. Can we go now?'

As we reversed down the drive, I thought I heard Jessica

whisper to her sister: 'He can't keep this up. We'll get him tomorrow for sure.'

Or perhaps it was just my imagination? Well, whatever – I've made up my mind. I've finished with the whistle and the scorecard. I reckon John McEnroe was right.

Umpiring is for jerks.

Points to remember:

1 The umpire is a jerk.
2 A father's responsibility is to look harassed and mumble a lot, not to referee fights.
3 Let the women interfere if they want to. They've had more practice than you.
4 Take away baseball bats, hammers and razor blades - especially from your wife - and let them all sort it out for themselves.
5 The umpire is a jerk.

Questions to think about:

- Who started it?
- Your children attack each other with Uzi sub-machine guns on the living room carpet while you are sitting down listening to Pavarotti. Should you (a) intervene or (b) turn up the volume on your headphones?
- What does 'confiscate' mean?

CHAPTER 19

Guess What?

The ultimate warning sign

So why do we do it? Why do men want to be fathers? Are there any pay-offs? Well, guess what? There are.

Accidents can happen

'Guess whaaa-aaat?'

Two words with a music of their own. When spoken by our three-year-old, Jessica, they are more like the lyrics of a short song which starts at A flat and ends on F sharp. It's a dreadful and dreaded anthem.

'Guess whaaa-aaat?'

'What, Jess?'

'I done wee in my bedwoom.'

She has too. Not on the cork either, but on the little square of carpet right in the centre of the room.

'Oh, Jessica . . . '

Sotto voce. 'Sowwy, Dad . . . '

My wife is out for the day. I have Jessica and an important deadline all to myself. I clean up the mess and return to work. Half an hour later, she's back.

'Guess whaaa-aaat?'

'What, Jess?'

'I made a really, really, really, big building in your bedwoom.'

'Did you, honey?'

'Come and see.'

I come and see. She really has made a really, really really big building in our bedroom – out of Helen's prized Wedgwood. All six pieces are precariously balanced on the edge of the dressing table. As we enter, the vibrations bring the whole construction crashing down.

There is a bit of yelling at this point. Jessica somehow sees herself as the victim of parental persecution and storms off to her bedroom, slamming the door.

I pick up the Wedgwood. Fortunately it landed on carpet and there are only a couple of chipped pieces. I go back to the study muttering half-formed threats and peace descends once more.

Don't get upset over trifles

For a while, anyway. 'Guess whaaa-aaat?'

'What, Jess?'

'I made some custard.'

Oh, my God. Stay calm. 'Did you, darling?'

'Come and see.'

Do I dare? We descend the steps, hand in hand, to the kitchen. It has snowed inside. There is a fine coating of white powder over all the floors, on the stove, on the breakfast bar and on top of the fridge. The kitchen workbench is a morass of yellowish sludge where she has added a little water to the recipe.

'Jessica!! What have you done?'

She gives me the little voice again: 'Sowwy, Daddy.'

'Did you make this mess?' Well, a stupid question really. She's already used the George Washington defence and confessed.

'I want to be fwends,' she sobs and rushes up to her bedroom, slamming the door.

I clean up the custard – a trifle messy, ho, ho – and return to work. I have barely sat down when I hear a little voice murmur to no one in particular. 'Guess whaaa-aaat?'

'WHAT HAVE YOU DONE?'

She's already crying, so I know it's a goodie. 'I don't want you to yell at me.'

'I'M NOT YELLING. WHAT HAVE YOU DONE, FOR GOD'S SAKE?'

'Pwuned the twees.'

Oh, no. Oh, please God, no. She saw me pruning the trees yesterday. Surely she didn't . . .

She did.

Simple really. Pair of scissors from the kitchen, half an hour alone in the garden and the six leafy young apple trees I planted the day before have been turned into divining rods.

I turn and glare at my daughter.

'I don't like you, I just like Mummy,' she says, as if this will somehow avert the righteous wrath that is about to descend.

It doesn't. She is severely chastened and put in her bedroom. As I go out she slams the door behind me.

I want my conviction squashed

After this, a whole afternoon goes by without further interruptions. Wait a minute. It's quiet out there, as John Wayne used to say before the Apaches attacked his wagon train. Too quiet.

I go downstairs. Jessica gives me a pixie smile. 'Guess whaaa-aaat?'

Oh, no. 'What?'

'I did dwawing.'

Yep. Sure did. All over my new book. It was a birthday

present, *Play Better Squash* by Chris Dittmar. You know, the other Chris Dittmar, the one with the green face and the purple beard.

'JESSICA!'

'I just want to be fwends.'

With friends like this, as they say . . .

She is again banished to her bedroom.

'This time,' I yell, on the way out, 'I'M SLAMMING THE DOOR!'

Guess what?

My wife is home in time for tea. As we sit around the dinner table that evening, the very image of domestic harmony, a stranger would never have guessed that two of the participants at the meal are bitter enemies.

Jessica shovels up a spoonful of peas. 'Guess what, Dad?'

Uh-oh. 'What, Jess?'

'Guess whaaa-aaat?'

'WHAT?'

A long sigh. 'I really, really, really, really love you.'

Gulp. At times like this, I can forgive her anything. Guess what? I really, really, really, really, love her too.

But don't ask me why.

CHAPTER 20

So You Want to Be a Parent?

A quiz to help you find out if you have the Right Stuff

They say the only people who know how to bring up children are the ones who don't have any. After all, it looks easy, doesn't it? Anything any calm, rational and reasonably intelligent adult should be able to manage.

Or is it?

I contend that being calm, rational and reasonably intelligent are not necessarily the best criteria for the job of being a father. There are other qualities that are more important. Do you have what it takes? Are you the Right Stuff?

Before you do anything rash, here's a little quiz to help you find out.

1 Are you a practising:

   a) nurse
   b) Catholic
   c) family counsellor
   d) masochist

2 What name do you usually answer to?

   a) Sir
   b) Your Worship
   c) O Fount of all Wisdom
   d) Hey you!

3 How would you best describe yourself?

  a) patient, kind and loving

  b) a bright and carefree kind of guy with an insatiable hunger for life

  c) a serene and spiritual man with a real sense of inner peace

  d) a drone who enjoys being bullied

4 What do you normally wear?

  a) a charcoal grey business suit and a powder blue silk shirt with button-down collar

  b) running shorts, headband and Reeboks

  c) Levis, a white T-shirt, Raybans and cowboy boots

  d) a tracksuit and a harassed expression

5 For relaxation I enjoy:

  a) listening to Mahler on my headphones

  b) playing tennis and swimming

  c) painting landscapes and making pottery

  d) refereeing fist fights and mending punctures

6 When it comes to decorating the home, I prefer:

  a) soft pastel shades that soothe the eye

  b) vibrant primary colours that make a strong statement about my character

  c) a combination of leather and pine with autumnal tonings on the walls

  d) Marmite on all the curtains and carpets

7 As a hobby, I like collecting:

  a) stamps

  b) rare coins

  c) antiques

  d) egg boxes and toilet roll holders

8 I would like to have children because:

a) I am a bubbly and creative person and I think it would be fun
b) It will fulfil me as a person
c) I want to share my wisdom with my offspring
d) I have led a terrible life and I deserve to suffer

9 Having children will be like:

a) *The Cosby Show*
b) *The Brady Bunch*
c) *Family Ties*
d) *Miami Vice*

10 I expect my children to:

a) show boundless curiosity and ask a lot of questions
b) imitate everything I do and look to me for guidance
c) be placid, lovable creatures who like to paint and draw
d) nag me endlessly about building a sandpit

11 If you get the chance to stay up till two in the morning, what do you prefer to do?

a) rage at a disco
b) go to dinner parties
c) go for long, romantic walks in the moonlight with your wife
d) try and convince a five-year-old that there is not a White Pointer on top of the wardrobe

12 What is your favourite topic of discussion in restaurants?

a) the theatre
b) the last country you've visited
c) the significance of the recent changes in Eastern Europe
d) potty training

13 What would you describe as your secret ambition in life?

a) to sail the world single-handed
b) to write a novel
c) to run your own business
d) to teach your three-year-old to share

14 Sometime in the future, I would like to:

a) travel the world
b) be able to go to restaurants three or four nights a week
c) take up yoga and learn another language
d) be blamed for a teenager's shortcomings – by the teenager

15 If you were re-incarnated as an animal in your next life, what would you like to be?

a) Mickey Rourke
b) a thoroughbred stallion running free in a wide, grassy paddock
c) a golden lion on the African veldt
d) a battered and weather-beaten humpback weighed down with lots of barnacles that won't let go

16 In your opinion, what was humanity's greatest invention?

a) the wheel
b) penicillin
c) the aeroplane
d) headphones

17 I am a generous person. I don't mind giving:

a) Ten per cent of my income to charity
b) Fifteen per cent of my income to my investment consultant
c) Thirty per cent of my income to the taxman
d) Ninety per cent of my income to the doctor, dentist, toyshop and the check-out girl at Sainsbury.

18 Which of the following courses have you attended?

a) parent-effectiveness training
b) baby massage
c) self-assertiveness training
d) an SAS survival course

19 Which of the following best describes your attitudes?

a) no one can tell me anything about how to raise children
b) I've read Doctor Spock and it sounds like there's nothing to it, really
c) I've read everything ever written about parenting and I'm pretty sure I could do a reasonably good job
d) I've read everything from *Parent Effectiveness Training* to the Book of Job and I still haven't got a clue

20 What are you most looking forward to in parenthood?

a) seeing their little eyes light up at Christmas
b) doing family things like going on picnics and going to fun parks
c) having someone to look after me in my old age
d) paying dental bills

Answers:

Award yourself two points for each correct answer.

1 (d), 1 point for (a): normal, healthy kids are sick eighty per cent of the time; **2** (d); **3** (d); **4** (d); **5** (d); **6** (d), 1 point for (c): dark colours hide dirty fingerprints; **7** (d); **8** (d); **9** (d), 1 point for any of the others, but only if you don't find them funny; **10** (d), 1 point for (a); **11** (d); **12** (d); **13** (d); **14** (d); **15** (d); **16** (d), 1 point for (b): you will be buying a lot, in one form or another, from your local pharmacy; **17** (d); **18** (d), 1 point for (c), 1 point for (a); **19** (d); **20** (d), take away 2 points if you answered (c), you poor, misguided fool.

Do you have the Right Stuff?

30–40 POINTS: You would make the perfect father: you enjoy being vilified, yelled at, and dominated. Go ahead, and have half a dozen. You'll love it.

20–30 POINTS: You should think long and hard before going ahead with fatherhood: you still have too many illusions. Perhaps you watched too many Fred MacMurray and Doris Day movies when you were a child.

10–20 POINTS: There are serious doubts about your suitability as a father; you may be one of those unusual types who enjoy unbroken sleep and not feeling tired all the time. If you do decide to go ahead, restrict yourself to just one or two, and space them a couple of decades apart.

LESS THAN 10 POINTS: Forget it.

Epilogue

Let's put all this in perspective. Being a father is not the most difficult thing you will ever do: not if you are Chris Bonnington, Sir Ranulph Fiennes or Frank Bruno. But if you are an ordinary bloke, you will be totally daunted when you finally come to realize the extent of the dilemma you have placed yourself in.

I've given you a few rules, but I must confess at this late stage that none of them are worth very much, since the rules vary from child to child. The only thing it is essential to remember is to retain your sense of humour. Without it, you have no chance. Unless you keep or develop a sense of humour, you will not be able to cope.

Laugh and the world laughs with you. Cry and your offspring will press home their advantage.

My wife and I hope that, after feeding the little monsters and buying them Barbie doll dream kitchens and ferrying them to and from Mick Jagger concerts (yes, I figure he may still be on his farewell tour in 2001), they will grow up to carry on our names, give us immortality, make my wife feel more feminine and me more like a man and prove to be a comfort to us in the winter of our years.

But I'm not counting on it.